ABRAH
2013

BIBLE
BOWLING

BIBLE
BOWLING

Sara Stoker

BARBOUR
PUBLISHING

Published by Barbour Publishing, Inc., P.O. Box 719, Uhrichsville, Ohio 44683, www.barbourbooks.com

Our mission is to publish and distribute inspirational products offering exceptional value and biblical encouragement to the masses.

ecpa Member of the
Evangelical Christian
Publishers Association

Printed in the United States of America.

Roll Your Way Through Fun Bible Trivia

Here's a new twist on Bible trivia—*Bible Bowling*, where you can earn pins, strikes, and spares according to your knowledge of scripture!

This fun Bible trivia challenge is organized into four "games" of twelve possible "frames" each. . .each frame featuring eleven questions. If you can answer each of the first ten questions correctly, you'll score a strike—but if you miss some questions, you still have a chance for a spare on the bonus eleventh question.

Each page includes a bowling score sheet for your convenience. Here's how to score bowling:

- For each frame in which you roll a strike, you get 10 points plus the value of the next two rolls—so if you roll three strikes in a row, you'll get 30 points in the first of the three frames.

- For each frame in which you pick up a spare, you get 10 points plus the value of the next roll—so, for example, if you roll a 9 on the next ball, your spare frame is worth 19 points.

- Each time you have an "open" frame—you don't roll a strike or a spare—you earn the number of pins you knocked over.

A perfect game of twelve consecutive strikes is worth 300 points. Think you can do that?

All questions are taken from the King James Version of the Bible, from both the Old and New Testaments.

Ready for some fun Bible trivia? Start rolling!

Contents

GAME 1

Game 1/Frame 1

Who committed the first murder?
 a. Adam
 b. Cain
 c. Lot
 d. Jacob

Who was Boaz's wife?
 a. Sarah
 b. Rebekah
 c. Ruth
 d. Hannah

What animal did God provide for a sacrifice in place of Abraham's son, Isaac?
 a. lamb   c. goat
 b. ram   d. toad

How many days was Jesus dead before rising up alive again?
 a. one day
 b. one week
 c. three days
 d. three weeks

Who built the ark for the coming flood?
 a. Noah
 b. Moses
 c. Samuel
 d. David

What is the last book in the Bible?
a. Malachi   c. Matthew
b. Genesis   d. Revelation 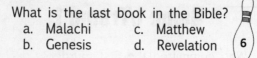 6

Which of Jesus' disciples was a former tax collector (also known as a publican)?
7
a. Peter   c. Judas
b. Paul   d. Matthew

What was the name of Eli the priest's grandson?
a. Phinehas   c. Ichabod 8
b. Hophni   d. Samuel

How many of Job's sons died during his trials?
9
a. all of his sons
b. one third of his sons
c. half of his sons
d. none of his sons

Who was the first martyr?
a. Phillip   c. Timothy
b. Stephen   d. Paul   10

SPARE:

Who said this: "How are the mighty fallen"?

a. King David (when King Saul died)
b. King Nebuchadnezzar (when Jerusalem was destroyed)
c. Queen Esther (when Haman plotted to kill all the Jews in the world)
d. King Herod (when he thought he killed baby king Jesus)

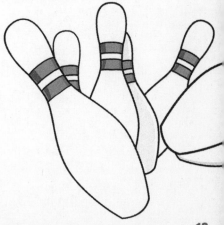

Game 1 / Frame 1

HOW MANY PINS
DID YOU KNOCK DOWN?

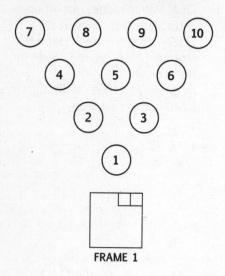

FRAME 1

Game 1/Frame 2

What clung to Paul as he carried logs for a fire?
   a. tarantula
   b. viper
   c. river rat
   d. green locust

How did Jael kill Israel's national enemy, Sisera?
   a. by hammering a tent peg through his skull
   b. by poisoning his wine during a feast
   c. by letting loose a herd of cattle to trample him
   d. by smothering him with animal hides

Who were the three friends of Job who dispersed faulty logic to him?
   a. Barak, Ben, Ebenezer
   b. Sheba, Bichri, Rogelim
   c. Barzillai, Mahanaim, Shemei
   d. Eliphaz, Bildad, and Zophar

After the fall of Babylon, in the book of Revelation, how long will the dragon be confined within the bottomless pit?
   a. 1 year   c. 100 years
   b. 10 years   d. 1,000 years

As Jesus was being arrested, one of the disciples chopped off what body part on the high priest's servant?

5

    a. his left hand
    b. his right ear
    c. his big nose
    d. his small finger

What common item did God use to unleash the plagues onto the Egyptians?

    a. a shepherd's rod
    b. an animal's jawbone
    c. a ram's horn
    d. a smooth pebble

6

In the armor-of-God analogy, what does the helmet represent?

7

    a. righteousness
    b. faith
    c. salvation
    d. truth

Who was Ishmael's mother?

    a. Bilhah
    b. Zilpah
    c. Hagar
    d. Sarah

8

What foolish thing did Isaiah say King Hezekiah did with the Babylonian envoys?

- a. poisoned their wine so as to only sicken them
- b. handed over the temple's treasuries instead of trusting God for deliverance
- c. refused them entry into Israel at their border
- d. showed them every single item in both his palace and the royal treasuries

9

What is the shortest verse in the New Testament?

- a. Jesus died
- b. Jesus wept
- c. Jesus came
- d. Jesus ate

10

SPARE:

Who said this: "Can the blind lead the blind?"

- a. Peter
- b. Paul
- c. John
- d. Jesus

Game 1 / Frame 2

HOW MANY PINS
DID YOU KNOCK DOWN?

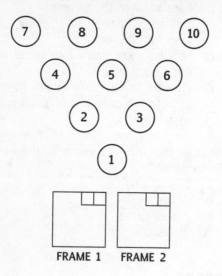

FRAME 1   FRAME 2

Game 1/Frame 3

Why did God allow the people of Ai to defeat and kill the Israelites during their first battle with Ai?
   a. the Israelites kept grumbling and finding fault with Moses
   b. some of the Israelite men married Canaanite women
   c. the Israelite Achan stole from the loot of a previous conquest and hid it
   d. the Egyptian Puar convinced the Israelites to return to Egypt and a safer life

Who was the last ruling king in the northern kingdom of Israel (or Samaria) before Assyria overtook it?
   a. Hoshea   c. Ahab
   b. Elah   d. Uriah

How many epistles did Paul write to Timothy?
   a. 0   c. 2
   b. 1   d. 3

Whom does God tempt?
   a. all nonbelievers
   b. just the murderers and other "hard-core" sinners
   c. just the atheists
   d. no one

What was Elisha doing at the time Elijah called him to follow him?

5

a. plowing a field with twelve teams of oxen
b. fighting the fearsome Assyrians as an Israelite soldier
c. helping a poor widow feed herself and her two sons
d. offering an unblemished lamb sacrifice to the Lord God

Who was the wicked man who plotted to annihilate every single Jew on earth?

6

a. Hal
b. Haran
c. Haman
d. Halaram

Why did King David murder Bathsheba's husband?

7

a. to hide the fact that the baby Bathsheba carried was his and not her husband's
b. he was found to be a traitor plotting David's assassination
c. his lineage was of Esau and a hated enemy since times of old
d. he was a foreigner in Israel's army and therefore not to be trusted

How does someone guarantee getting into heaven?
   a. believe in Jesus and pray and read the Bible regularly
   b. believe in Jesus and do good things for others regularly
   c. believe in Jesus and go to church regularly
   d. believe in Jesus and nothing else

8

In the seven letters to the seven churches, which church did God find to be dead?
9
   a. Sardis   c. Laodicea
   b. Philadelphia d. Ephesus

When Jesus died, how many pieces was the temple curtain torn into?
   a. two   c. seven
   b. four   d. eleven

10

SPARE:
Who said this: "Let us make man in our image"?
   a. a man   c. Satan
   b. an angel d. God

Game 1 / Frame 3

HOW MANY PINS
DID YOU KNOCK DOWN?

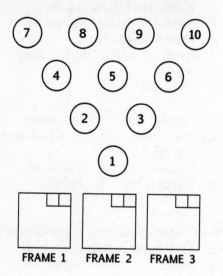

FRAME 1   FRAME 2   FRAME 3

Game 1/Frame 4

Who was Paul's teacher in the Law before he came to Christ?
  a. Rabbi Caiaphas
  b. Rabbi Gamaliel
  c. Rabbi Annas
  d. Rabbi Zerah

Who was Esau's father?
  a. Isaac
  b. Jacob
  c. Moses
  d. Abraham

Which famous prophet had the vision of four wheels covered with eyes?
  a. Isaiah
  b. Jeremiah
  c. Daniel
  d. Ezekiel

What are some characteristics of godly wisdom?
  a. divinity, higher reality, and spirituality
  b. factual, scientific, and error-free
  c. pureness, peacefulness, and no favoritism
  d. technological, useful, and logical

5 According to the Law, which of the following would be considered clean?
a. horse   c. cow
b. camel   d. rabbit

6 What did Elijah look like?
a. hairy man with a leather belt around his waist
b. bald man with leather sandals on his feet
c. fat man with a leather coat around his body
d. short man with a leather satchel over his shoulder

7 In what city was Peter lodging when Cornelius's servants visited him?
a. Jerusalem   c. Caesarea
b. Joppa   d. Philippi

8 In the parable of the soils, how many soil types were represented?
a. two   c. six
b. four   d. eight

9 What nation came from the incestuous relationship between Lot and his older daughter?
a. Moabites   c. Amorites
b. Hittites   d. Ammonites

What was Martha's "beef" with her sister, Mary?

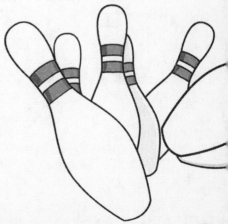

a. Mary sat like a guest instead of helping with the dinner preparations
b. Mary nitpicked and complained about everything Martha was doing
c. Mary was clumsy and was more of a hindrance than a help
d. Mary claimed to be sick again so she could get out of helping

SPARE:

Who said this: "What is truth?"

a. Peter   c. Pan
b. Paul   d. Pilate

Game 1 / Frame 4

HOW MANY PINS DID YOU KNOCK DOWN?

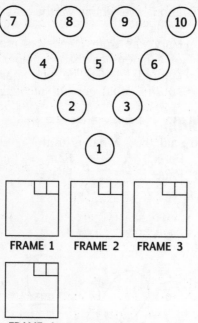

7 8 9 10

4 5 6

2 3

1

FRAME 1   FRAME 2   FRAME 3

FRAME 4

Game 1/Frame 5

What was Queen Esther's "trump card" to thwart the annihilation of her Jewish people?
  a. no one knew she was independently wealthy and could purchase their freedom
  b. no one knew she had a massive army at her command
  c. no one knew that she was of Nebuchadnezzar's royal lineage
  d. no one knew that she was Jewish herself

What did Pharaoh's troubling dreams consist of during Joseph's time?
  a. steeds and wheat
  b. swine and barley
  c. kine and corn
  d. fowl and oats

What is faith?
  a. warm fuzzy feelings necessary to avoid depression
  b. concrete scientific facts with plenty of evidence to back them up
  c. being sure of what is hoped for and certain of what is unseen
  d. abstract dreams to cling to when one cannot get very far in the real world

What was the name of Timothy's mother?

a. Lois
b. Eunice
c. Lydia
d. Shannon

4

In Moses' first authorized census of the twelve tribes, which tribe was the largest?

5

a. Manasseh
b. Dan
c. Benjamin
d. Judah

What was Jesus known to go about doing in every city He entered?

a. preaching and healing
b. pointing out the Pharisees' hypocrisy
c. pointing out the people's sins
d. giving the rabbinic blessing on the children

6

During King Ahab's reign, what was the punishment a prophet decreed because a disobedient man didn't strike him as commanded?

7

a. he would be devoured by a lion
b. he would be bitten by a viper
c. he would be drowned in a shipwreck
d. he would be suffocated by an animal hide

Why did Deborah, a woman, accompany Israel's army general, Barak, during a military campaign?

- a. because he was an invalid
- b. because he was a coward
- c. because he was her father
- d. because she was a God-fearing Law abider

8

What was Aquila and Pricilla's occupation?

- a. sellers of purple dye
- b. jewelry makers
- c. tentmakers
- d. sellers of eye salve

9

Who is the only person who lived after the flood and who never died?

- a. Enoch
- b. Esau
- c. Elisha
- d. Elijah

10

SPARE:

Who said this: "Ask, and it shall be given you"?

- a. Paul
- b. Joshua
- c. Jesus
- d. Abraham

Game 1 / Frame 5

HOW MANY PINS
DID YOU KNOCK DOWN?

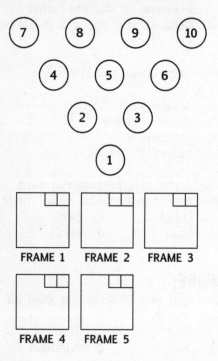

FRAME 1   FRAME 2   FRAME 3

FRAME 4   FRAME 5

Game 1/Frame 6

1) Who was Philemon?
- a. slave owner
- b. runaway slave
- c. common soldier
- d. army commander

How many sons did Leah's handmaiden, Zilpah, bear Jacob?
- a. 2
- b. 3
- c. 6
- d. 12

2

3) How long did the Ephesian silversmiths' unruly and almost lethal riot last?
- a. five minutes
- b. two hours
- c. half a day
- d. one full week

How did David take down the giant named Goliath?
- a. with a club
- b. with a nail
- c. with a stone
- d. with a sword

4

How many books are in the New Testament?
- a. eighteen
- b. twenty-seven
- c. thirty-nine
- d. forty-five

5

How should someone respond to beautiful things in nature, such as a gorgeous sunset?

a. worship it because it is an object God created
b. worship God because He created it
c. study it intently so that one can explain the phenomenon if asked
d. ignore it because life is too short to waste time on unprofitable things

6

What did Samuel call the place where the Lord thundered and smote the Philistines?

7

a. Ebenezer   c. Ichabod
b. Jabba   d. Zedad

How has Jesus Christ changed over the years?

a. He has become more lenient and looks the other way over accidental sins
b. He has become harsher and angrier with the more serious sins
c. He has become more understanding and forgiving with sin in general
d. He has not changed but remains the same yesterday, today, and forevermore

8

How long did it take for God to create the universe and everything in it?

a. 1 day   c. 7 days
b. 6 days   d. 10 days

Which bird did God create to be extremely foolish?

a. owl   c. stork
b. seagull   d. ostrich

SPARE:

Who said this: "My soul doth magnify the Lord"?

a. Miriam   c. Mary
b. Hannah   d. Elizabeth

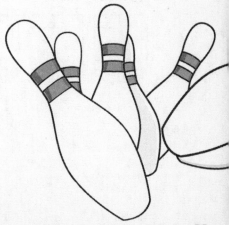

Game 1 / Frame 6

HOW MANY PINS DID YOU KNOCK DOWN?

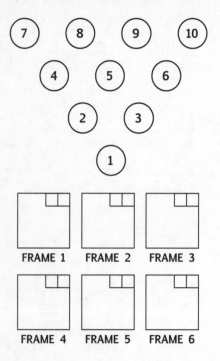

Game 1/Frame 7

What does Taberah mean?
a. the place of burning because God scorched dead the complainers
b. the place of drowning because God caused the Jordan river to overflow
c. the place of contentment because God fed Israel after three days of no food
d. the place of laughter because God gave Israel the ability to forgive and forget

What was the first thing Jesus did when the Pharisees and teachers made a public spectacle of a woman caught in adultery?
a. yelled at the woman
b. yelled at the Pharisees and teachers
c. rolled his eyes and ignored them
d. scribbled in the sand and ignored them

Who ripped up the written words of God and threw them into a fire?
a. Jeremiah the prophet
b. Elishama the scribe
c. Jehudi the priest
d. Jehoiakim the king

What did the Babylonian king Evilmerodach do to Jehoiachin, the exiled king of Judah?
a. tortured him by cutting off one body part a week until he died
b. only fed him once a week, and soon he died
c. impaled him on a fifteen-foot stake, and he died
d. released him from prison and dined with him until he died

How often should one pray?
a. only in public where it is considered legitimate
b. only when led by the Spirit
c. always
d. never

What were the twelve words inscribed on New Jerusalem's city gates?
a. the names of the tribes of Israel
b. the names of the apostles
c. curses
d. commandments

While Joseph was in prison, which two Egyptian officials told him their dreams?
a. the butler and the baker
b. the baker and the shoemaker
c. the shoemaker and the gardener
d. the gardener and the butler

Among the many things Jesus rightfully claimed to be, which of the following is one of them?
- a. manna of strength
- b. bread of life
- c. wine of vitality
- d. milk of eternity

8

What was the point of sewing fringes/tassels on the hems of all of the Israelite clothes?
- a. to start a new fashion statement among the Canaanite neighbors
- b. as an outward sign of how pious Israelites really were
- c. to remind the Israelites of the need for obedience and holy living to God
- d. to copy the clothes Moses wore, out of deep respect for him

9

Why did God save Noah and his family?
- a. Noah was already kind to the animals
- b. Noah was already practically perfect
- c. Noah found grace in the Lord
- d. Noah asked God to be saved and He heard him

10

SPARE:

Who said this: "Render therefore unto Caesar the things which are Caesar's; and unto God the things that are God's"?

a. Caesar
b. Jesus
c. Pilate
d. Paul

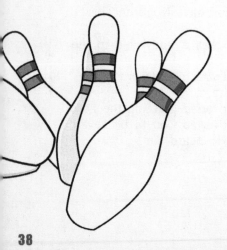

Game 1 / Frame 7

HOW MANY PINS
DID YOU KNOCK DOWN?

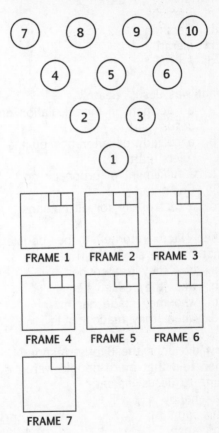

Game 1/Frame 8

Which Levite clan was assigned to carry the sacred objects in the tabernacle?
1
a. Kohath
b. Gershon
c. Merari
d. Aaron

What was Jesus' death?
a. an accident in miscalculation on Jesus' part
b. a tragedy of ignorance on the rulers' part
c. a fulfillment of prophecy on God's part
2
d. a fact of life for all humans

When Naomi returned to her people, what did she scold them about?
a. how they treated her
3
b. what they called her
c. who they made her marry
d. where they made her live

How did John the Baptist respond when told that more people were going to Jesus instead?
a. happy
b. sad
c. angry
4
d. confused

40

Who was the prophet Samuel's mother?
- a. Sarah
- b. Rebekah
- c. Ruth
- d. Hannah

What were Paul and Silas doing while imprisoned in the Philippian jail?
- a. sobbing and worrying
- b. worrying and praying
- c. praying and singing
- d. singing and laughing

What is the shortest book in the Old Testament?
- a. Amos
- b. Obadiah
- c. Jonah
- d. Malachi

In the end-time, how many trumpets of judgment will there be?
- a. 2
- b. 3
- c. 7
- d. 12

Where does temptation come from?
- a. God
- b. Satan
- c. corrupt people
- d. our own desires

How did King Solomon solve the dispute between the two prostitute mothers concerning one baby who was smothered to death?

a. he arbitrarily gave the baby to one of the mothers
b. he threatened to cut the live baby in half, giving one half to each mother
c. he took the baby and raised him in the royal palace
d. he did nothing because he dismissed the case as foolish women's nonsense

SPARE:

Who said this: "Cry aloud: for he [Baal] is a god; either he is talking, or he is pursuing, or he is in a journey, or peradventure he sleepeth, and must be awaked"?

a. Elijah
b. Baalek
c. Jacob
d. Jesus

Game 1 / Frame 8

HOW MANY PINS DID YOU KNOCK DOWN?

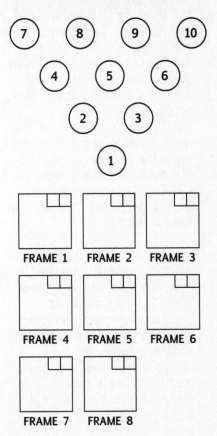

Game 1/Frame 9

What was the stark difference between the prayers of the Pharisee and the publican?
 a. the Pharisee's prayer was full of self-righteous arrogance, while the publican's was humble
 b. the Pharisee's prayer included the correct respectful words, while the publican spoke the wrong words
 c. the publican's prayer was too quiet to be reasonably heard, while the Pharisee spoke up
 d. the publican's prayer was too sinful to be accepted in the temple, while the Pharisee spoke holy words

Who has committed enough sin to bar them from entering heaven?
 a. everyone who has ever lived except for sinless Jesus
 b. everyone who has ever been a murderer, rapist, or committed another serious sin
 c. everyone who has ever been really evil, like Hitler
 d. everyone who has ever cut someone off in traffic

3 When Jacob finally met Pharaoh face-to-face, what did he do?
    a. kick him   c. curse him
    b. kiss him   d. bless him

How did God first speak to young Samuel?
    a. by giving him prophetic dreams for three nights in a row
    b. by audibly calling his name during the night
    c. by appearing like an angel during the nighttime sacrifice
    d. by setting a bush on fire without burning it to the ground

4

How did the men of Benjamin's tribe choose their wives during the Judges' era?
    a. by killing wild lions and after skinning them, wore their hides to woo the girls
    b. by hiding in the vineyard and when they passed by, chasing them down
    c. by voluntarily enslaving themselves to their future father-in-laws
    d. by contesting each other through riddles and wealth accumulation

5

Late in the day of Jesus' resurrection, He met up with two followers on the road to where?

a. Joppa   c. Ephesus
b. Jerusalem   d. Emmaus

6

What was Esther's Jewish name?

a. Haran   c. Hadassah
b. Hannah   d. Hamash

7

In the New Jerusalem, what are the city gates made out of?

a. gold   c. onyx
b. pearl   d. ruby

8

On which day of creation did God create the little goldfish?

a. third   c. fifth
b. fourth   d. sixth

9

What physical ailment accompanied the direct communication between Saul and Jesus?

a. he became blind
b. he became deaf
c. he became mute
d. he became paralyzed

10

SPARE:

Who said this: "We have no king but Caesar"?

a. slaves   c. Jews
b. foreigners   d. soldiers

Game 1 / Frame 9

HOW MANY PINS DID YOU KNOCK DOWN?

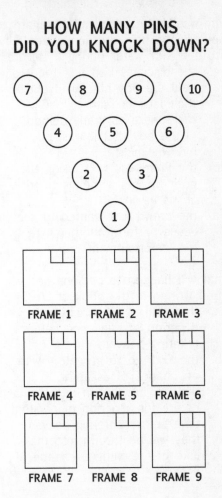

Game 1/Frame 10

Why was Jesus dismayed in regard to the epileptic boy who sometimes fell into a fire or water during a seizure?

a. the disciples had first tried to heal the boy but failed due to their lack of faith

b. there were so many demons in the boy that it was overwhelming

c. the Pharisees were using the poor boy as a means to trick Jesus again

d. the crowd just wanted to see Jesus perform another miracle for "entertainment"

What will happen to persons not found written in the book of life?

a. they will go to purgatory for a period of penitence before entering heaven

b. they will go to purgatory with no chance of escaping

c. they will be thrown into the lake of fire for a period of penitent time before entering heaven

d. they will be thrown into the lake of fire with no chance of escaping

Where did the prophet Samuel find David so he could be anointed the next king?

- a. eating dinner with his father and brothers
- b. eating dinner by himself
- c. shepherding his father's sheep with his brothers
- d. shepherding his father's sheep by himself

3

What was unusual about the faces of the four winged creatures in Ezekiel's vision?

- a. each one had one horn in its forehead (like a unicorn)
- b. each one had seven eyes (the center one was bigger than the others)
- c. each one had four faces (human, lion, ox, eagle)
- d. each one had three mouths (human, animal, fish)

4

How was a bitter, undrinkable spring of water made pure?

- a. some salt was thrown in it
- b. a prayerful incantation was uttered over it
- c. some people dug a canal from another spring to it
- d. some water was taken from it and thrown over the people's shoulders

5

For seven years, what did God condemn King Nebuchadnezzar to because of his pride?
a. he became a POW to the hated enemy Egyptians
b. he became a slave among his own people
c. he became like a wild animal and ate grass
d. he became a bed-ridden invalid who never left his palace

6

What was the early Christian sect originally called?

7
a. the Way   c. the Life
b. the Truth   d. the Jesusonians

What forbidden food did Jonathan eat after a successful battle with the Philistines?
a. raisins   c. milk
b. honey   d. wine

8

Why do we need to put on the whole armor of God?
a. so we can correctly point out the errors and injustices around us
b. so we can better pray and focus on godly matters
c. so we can withstand in the evil day
d. so we can be guaranteed of getting into heaven

9

In whose house was Peter staying when Cornelius visited him?
a. Paul the tentmaker
b. Simon the tanner
c. James the shepherd
d. Joseph the carpenter

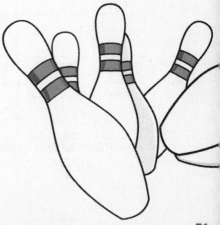

SPARE:

Who said this: "For whatsoever a man soweth, that shall he also reap"?
a. Jesus   c. Samuel
b. Jacob   d. Paul

Game 1 / Frame 10

HOW MANY PINS DID YOU KNOCK DOWN?

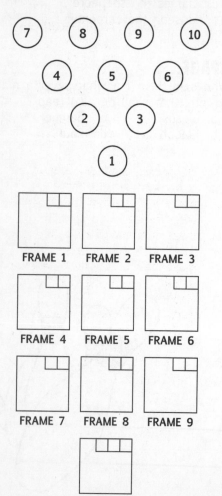

Game 1/Bonus Ball 1

Play only if you rolled a spare or strike in Frame 10.

1. How many books are in the Bible?
   a. 27
   b. 39
   c. 66
   d. 124

2. Which church was found faithful in Revelation?
   a. Sardis
   b. Philadelphia
   c. Ephesus
   d. Laodicea

3. What unnatural thing did Gideon ask God to do with the fleece?
   a. make it wet when the ground was dry and vice versa
   b. make it black when it had been white and vice versa
   c. make it into a lion's skin when it had been a sheepskin and vice versa
   d. make it huge when it was small and vice versa

4. Which of Noah's sons became the father of Canaan?
   a. Cain
   b. Shem
   c. Japheth
   d. Ham

Who was the very first human that God created?

5
a. Adam   c. Noah
b. Abel   d. Abraham

Why do believers call the Last Supper "the Last Supper"? It was:
a. the last meal all twelve disciples would eat with Jesus before He was crucified
b. the last meal all twelve disciples would eat with Jesus before He ascended

6
c. the last meal Jesus would eat on earth until His kingdom is ushered in on earth
d. the last meal Jesus would eat on earth ever again

Who beguiled King Solomon into worshipping foreign false gods?

7
a. his foreign cupbearer
b. his foreign wives
c. his own children
d. his own political advisors

How many years was the crippled woman in a bent-over position, unable to stand up straight, before Jesus healed her?

8
a. 4 years   c. 18 years
b. 9 years   d. 43 years
                  (her whole life)

In which city were Christians first called "Christians"?

(9)
   a. Jerusalem   c. Ephesus
   b. Corinth   d. Antioch

What was unusual about King Nebuchadnezzar's request to have his dream interpreted?

   a. they had to first translate the dream into their language
   b. they had to first guess what the dream was about

(10)

   c. they had to first offer one of their sons for sacrifice
   d. they had to first pay money for the honor of interpreting the dream

SPARE:

Who said this: "Great is the wrath of the LORD that is kindled against us, because our fathers have not hearkened unto the words of this book"?

   a. King Josiah
   b. Queen Esther
   c. the priest Hilkiah
   d. the prophet Isaiah

Game 1/Bonus Ball 2

Play only if you rolled strikes on Frame 10 and Bonus Ball 1.

1. What was Mordecai's relation to Queen Esther?
   a. brother
   b. father
   c. uncle
   d. cousin

2. What object was found in Benjamin's sack when the eleven brothers were on their way back home with grain the second time?
   a. a gold signet ring
   b. a silver cup
   c. a bronze statue
   d. a brass pot

3. Who did Paul choose to go with on his second missionary trip?
   a. Silas
   b. Barnabas
   c. John
   d. Timothy

4. What did God do on the seventh day of creation?
   a. rested
   b. critiqued
   c. recreated
   d. analyzed

Which gospel was written as an orderly account of historical facts on Jesus?

5
a. Matthew   c. Luke
b. Mark   d. John

How did the King Herod who persecuted the early church die?
a. heart attack
b. eaten up by worms
c. fatal wounds during a battle
d. old age

6

When Jesus prayed in the Garden of Gethsemane, His sweat became like what?

7
a. water   c. blood
b. oil   d. perfume

What did Ishmael and ten rebels do to King Nebuchadnezzar's appointed governor?
a. ridiculed him
b. tortured him
c. enslaved him
d. assassinated him

8

How many epistles did Paul write to Silas?

9
a. 0   c. 2
b. 1   d. 3

During King Josiah's reign, what did the high priest Hilkiah stumble upon in the temple?

a. Aaron's staff that had budded
b. the original stone Ten Commandments
c. the book of the Law
d. the original ark of the Lord

10

Game 2/Frame 1

What are parables?
- a. a person walking parallel to someone else
- b. the smallest coin denomination used in Corinth and Nazareth
- c. an instrument of torture used by the Roman soldiers
- d. short stories illustrating biblical truths

Why were some of the tribes of Israel ready to engage in civil war so soon after entering the Promised Land?
- a. they jumped to the wrong conclusion regarding the building of a second altar
- b. they did not like how small their land allotments were
- c. they had a history of unruly rebels within their ranks
- d. their Philistine neighbors bribed them into warring with their own kinsmen

How long did Paul stay in Corinth?
- a. one and a half days
- b. one and a half weeks
- c. one and a half months
- d. one and a half years

How was a pot of stew that was accidentally poisoned miraculously fixed?
   a. by pouring it onto the altar of the Lord's temple
   b. by adding some flour to it
   c. by using some of it to water the olive tree grove
   d. it was never fixed so they had to throw out the poisoned stew

4

What common item did God use to allow Samson to kill 1,000 Philistines?
   a. ram's horn
   b. donkey's jawbone
   c. lion's tailbone
   d. camel's skull

5

Exactly how is a believer's salvation obtained?
   a. through silver and gold
   b. through daily deeds of goodwill
   c. through Jesus' blood
   d. through at least one of our parent's Christian faith

6

In Moses' first authorized census of the twelve tribes of Israel, which tribe was the smallest?
   a. Manasseh
   b. Dan
   c. Benjamin
   d. Judah

7

What was so special about
Bartimaeus?
   a. he was a blind beggar asking
       Jesus to give him back his sight
   b. he was a Roman centurion
       asking Jesus to walk again
   c. he was a rich Jew asking Jesus
       for eternal life
   d. he was a Samaritan leper who
       remembered to thank Jesus

What did Jesus do when He found a
mature fig tree with no figs on it?
   a. cursed it and the tree withered
   b. blessed it and the tree
       produced fruit
   c. scolded it and the tree dropped
       its leaves
   d. ignored it and the tree shook
       violently

In the Garden of Eden, which animal
did Satan appear as when he
deceived Eve?
   a. spider   c. serpent
   b. lizard   d. mouse

SPARE:
Who said this: "Let my people go"?
   a. Jeremiah through Baruch
   b. God through Moses
   c. King David through Joab
   d. God through Jesus

Game 2 / Frame 1

HOW MANY PINS
DID YOU KNOCK DOWN?

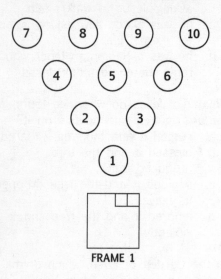

FRAME 1

Game 2/Frame 2

1. What was the name of Timothy's grandmother?
   a. Eunice   c. Deborah
   b. Lois   d. Lydia

2. Where did Rahab hide the two spies?
   a. with the stalks of drying flax on her roof
   b. in a well that was dry
   c. in the stables with the camels and donkeys
   d. in the walls because her house was in the city wall

3. At what time of day did the Pharisee Nicodemus visit Jesus?
   a. sunrise   c. late afternoon
   b. midday   d. after dark

4. What horrible thing did Joseph's brothers do to him?
   a. shaved off only half his beard and head of hair
   b. sold him as a slave to a passing traders' caravan
   c. chopped off both of his hands
   d. plucked out one of his eyes

How did King Herod respond to some foreigners' desire to meet the newborn king of the Jews?

5

a. he was enthusiastic
b. he was fearful
c. he was curious
d. he was indifferent

When Israel's King Ahaziah fell through the latticework of an upper room and was seriously injured, whom did he turn to for healing?

6

a. the Lord God
b. Elijah, prophet of God
c. Baalzebub, god of Ekron
d. no one, he figured the injuries were too hopeless to cure

How was God's covenant promise to Abraham and his descendants shown?

7

a. everyone must wear tassels on the end of all of their garments
b. every female must never cut her hair
c. every male must be circumcised
d. every male must never consume grape products (raisins, grapes, wine)

What is one main difference between the Sadducees and the Pharisees?
 a. Sadducees believed in a resurrection, Pharisees did not
 b. Pharisees believed in a resurrection, Sadducees did not
 c. Sadducees believed a Messiah would come, Pharisees did not
 d. Pharisees believed a Messiah would come, Sadducees did not

What physical handicap did Jacob's father develop in old age?
 a. blindness   c. paralysis
 b. deafness   d. a limp

The "crime" posted over Jesus as He hung on the cross was translated into which three languages?
 a. Aramaic, Latin, and Greek
 b. Latin, Greek, and Hebrew
 c. Aramaic, Hebrew, and Latin
 d. Greek, Egyptian, and Aramaic

SPARE:

With what were these words written: "Mene, Mene, Tekel, Upharsin"?
 a. the staff of Moses
 b. the pen of Paul
 c. the hand of Nebuchadnezzar
 d. the finger of God

Game 2 / Frame 2

HOW MANY PINS
DID YOU KNOCK DOWN?

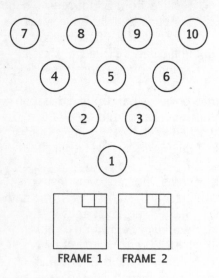

FRAME 1   FRAME 2

Game 2/Frame 3

1 What crime did Potiphar's wife accuse Joseph of committing?
- a. raping her
- b. starving her
- c. abusing her
- d. torturing her

Where did Apollos hail from?
- a. Bethlehem, Judea
- b. Rome, Italy
- c. Corinth, Greece
- d. Alexandria, Egypt

2

3 Who was the evil queen who ruled Judah for seven years?
- a. Queen Athaliah
- b. Queen Jezebel
- c. Queen Esther
- d. Queen Vashti

Which law of physics did God defy when He called Moses to lead His people?
- a. a flock of sheep started mooing like cows
- b. a desert bush was on fire but did not burn up
- c. the skies turned bright yellow instead of blue
- d. the waters parted to make a dry path

5 Who was the baby that leaped inside his mother's womb at the sound of Mary's voice?
   a. Jesus
   b. James
   c. John the Baptist
   d. Joseph

When should we obey our bosses at work?
   a. when they are looking
   b. when they are worth our time
   c. never if they are untrustworthy **6**
   d. always, whether they deserve it or not

7 What happened when a man's ax head fell off into the Jordan River while he was chopping down trees?
   a. it was never seen again
   b. a big fish scooped it up and brought it to the shore
   c. a large bird dove into the waters and rescued it
   d. a stick was thrown in and caused the metal ax head to float to the surface

What was the relationship between James and John?
   a. they were cousins
   b. they were brothers **8**
   c. they were father and son
   d. they were uncle and nephew

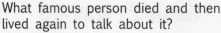

9 What famous person died and then lived again to talk about it?

    a. Muhammad   c. Gandhi

    b. Buddha   d. Jesus

How did the nearby Gibeonites deceive Joshua into an alliance God strictly forbade?

    a. they disguised themselves as travelers from a far country

    b. they ambushed the Israelites while two of them pretended to make peace

    c. they enticed the Israelites to marry their foreign women

    d. they bribed a few high-ranking Israelite officers into signing a secret peace treaty

10

SPARE:

Who said this: "Glory to God in the highest, and on earth peace, good will toward men"?

    a. Levites

    b. prophets

    c. Jesus

    d. angels

Game 2 / Frame 3

HOW MANY PINS
DID YOU KNOCK DOWN?

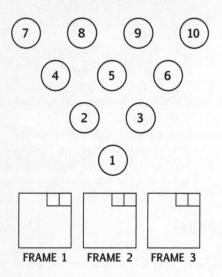

FRAME 1   FRAME 2   FRAME 3

Game 2/Frame 4

1. How did the busy disciples accept the parents bringing their children to Jesus for a blessing?
   a. they welcomed them with open arms
   b. they told them to go away
   c. they ignored them with forced indifference
   d. they responded warily as any one of them could try to assassinate Jesus

2. What was the name of Noah's boat? It was called the
   a. *Clipper*
   b. *QE2*
   c. *Ark*
   d. *Titanic*

3. What was Luke's profession?
   a. doctor
   b. lawyer
   c. soldier
   d. tax collector

4. On which day of creation did God create the Big Dipper?
   a. third
   b. fourth
   c. fifth
   d. sixth

Why didn't God allow Moses to lead
the Israelites into the Promised Land?

- a. he was too old—he was already
  120 years old
- b. it was punishment for not
  believing in God's power over
  the complaining Israelites
- c. Joshua needed to start gaining
  experience as God's number-one
  man
- d. it was a lesson to teach Moses
  who was ultimately in charge of
  his life

5

What did Jesus say when He stood
before Herod during His trial?

- a. He answered all questions with
  one- or two-word answers
- b. all answers focused on how
  Jesus was of the heavenly
  kingdom
- c. He told parables as they "heard
  but with no understanding"
- d. He spoke not one word

6

Who penned these words to this
psalm: "As the hart panteth after the
water brooks, so panteth my soul
after thee, O God"?

- a. David
- b. Moses
- c. the sons of Korah
- d. anonymous

7

How did the men of Gilead determine their enemy, Ephraim, from others?
a. by how they walked
b. by what type of cloak they wore
c. by the type of weapon they carried
d. by their accent

8

Who is the Lamb's wife?
a. the twelve tribes of Israel
b. the faithful prophets
c. the believers living in the New Jerusalem
d. there really is no such thing

9

For how many days did Elisha reluctantly allow fifty strong men to futilely search for Elijah's missing body?
a. three days
b. thirty days
c. they never bothered searching for his body
d. they kept up the search until they eventually died themselves

10

SPARE:
Who said this: "Come now, and let us reason together"?
a. God   c. Moses
b. Jesus   d. Abraham

Game 2 / Frame 4

HOW MANY PINS DID YOU KNOCK DOWN?

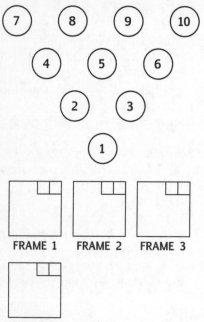

FRAME 1   FRAME 2   FRAME 3

FRAME 4

Game 2/Frame 5

What did King Nebuchadnezzar find peculiar about the men he ordered thrown into the furnace?
- a. they were singing and praying
- b. they were walking around
- c. they were laughing at the king
- d. they were reading scrolls

What finally forced the dishonest judge to administer justice to a wronged widow?
- a. her perseverance in asking for justice
- b. her bribe of twenty shekels
- c. her influential friends
- d. the death of a colleague

What happened to the bullock Elijah sacrificed, after he carefully drenched it with lots of water?
- a. nothing, because it was too wet
- b. it was completely consumed by fire from heaven, along with the wood and stones
- c. it appeared to come to life by rising to its feet for a few minutes
- d. it spoke

Exactly what died during the flood if it was not on the ark?
  a. every human being in the whole region
  b. every living creature in the whole region
  c. every human being in the whole world
  d. every living creature in the whole world

Who carried the cross while Jesus was led to the place of crucifixion?
  a. Jesus himself
  b. Peter of Galilee
  c. Simon of Cyrene
  d. a soldier of Rome

What is the most unruly part of the body?
  a. the mind   c. the tongue
  b. the eyes   d. the hands

Where did a woman hide the two messengers when King David was fleeing from his son, Absalom?
  a. with the stalks of drying flax on her roof
  b. in a well that was dry
  c. in the stables with the camels and donkeys
  d. in the walls because her house was in the city wall

What did Pilate do upon hearing that Jesus hailed from Galilee?
  a. shuttled Him over to King Herod because Galilee was in his jurisdiction
  b. threw Him in prison because Galileans were known as murderers and rebels
  c. had Him flogged to try and change His answer
  d. apologized and gave Him some food and a new change of clothes

8

Where did Barnabas hail from?
  a. Lystra   c. Cyprus
  b. Tarsus   d. Ephesus

9

Who can be saved?
  a. only the people who obey the Bible's commands regularly
  b. only the people who have not committed an evil act
  c. only the people who genuinely help others regularly
  d. every person who calls upon the name of the Lord

10

SPARE:

Who said this: "Be ye angry, and sin not"?
  a. Paul   c. Moses
  b. Jesus   d. Abraham

Game 2 / Frame 5

HOW MANY PINS DID YOU KNOCK DOWN?

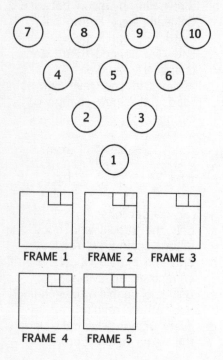

FRAME 1   FRAME 2   FRAME 3

FRAME 4   FRAME 5

Game 2/Frame 6

Of the ten virgins waiting for the bridegroom, why were five accused of being foolish?

1

    a. they did not come prepared with extra oil
    b. they did come with a gift for the bridegroom
    c. they did not come with a second cloak
    d. they did not come wearing the required perfumes for a wedding

Who was Jude a brother to?

    a. Peter   c. James
    b. John   d. Matthew

2

What was King Solomon's answer to God's question: "What do you wish from Me?"

3

    a. health
    b. wealth
    c. his enemies' death
    d. wisdom

According to the Law, which of the following would be considered clean?

    a. lobster   c. salmon
    b. shrimp   d. clams

4

During Isaiah's time, when King Hezekiah was deathly ill, what sign did God do to prove He would give the king fifteen more years to live?

5

a. the sun stood still for one whole day
b. the sun's shadow moved ten steps backward on the sundial
c. the sun turned dark at midday
d. the sun did nothing extraordinary, it was the moon that turned bloodred

How did God prove to the murmuring Israelites that He chose Aaron to be the high priest?

a. the sky opened up in hail and thunder
b. his branch rod budded and blossomed

6

c. it snowed for almost half a day in the wilderness
d. an earthquake split the Israelite camp in half

After the angels blow their trumpets, how many God-appointed witnesses will there be?

7

a. 0   c. 2
b. 1   d. 3

What were the twelve names inscribed onto New Jerusalem's twelve foundations?
   a. the twelve apostles of Jesus
   b. the twelve tribes of Israel
   c. the twelve sons of David
   d. the twelve cities of the early church

8

What was the total number of wives and concubines that King Solomon acquired?

9

   a. 10   c. 1,000
   b. 100   d. 10,000

What happened to the first two army captains and one hundred soldiers who failed to show proper humility before Elijah when they were to take him in for questioning?
   a. God burned them to a crisp
   b. God plagued them with leprosy
   c. God trampled them under a herd of wild horses
   d. God crushed them beneath an avalanche of falling cliff rocks

10

SPARE:
Who said this: "As ye would that men should do to you, do ye also to them likewise"?
   a. Peter   c. James
   b. Paul   d. Jesus

Game 2 / Frame 6

HOW MANY PINS DID YOU KNOCK DOWN?

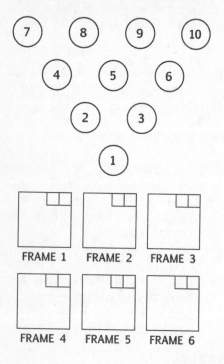

FRAME 1 FRAME 2 FRAME 3

FRAME 4 FRAME 5 FRAME 6

Game 2/Frame 7

1. Who initiated the citywide riot in Ephesus?
   a. Peter
   b. Paul
   c. the city rulers
   d. Demetrius

2. What was the Jewish leaders' biggest problem with Jesus' miraculous healings?
   a. the healings were done with official approval
   b. the healings were done on the Sabbath
   c. the healings were done to known sinners and tax collectors
   d. the healings were done as a means of showing off

3. What does *Marah* mean?
   a. "what is it" to describe the bread from heaven each morning
   b. "refreshing" to describe the date trees at the oasis
   c. "bitter" to describe the only available water in three days
   d. "hunger" to describe their countenance at having nothing to eat in days

How did the Philistines return the stolen ark?
a. in a cart pulled by mother cows who walked away from their newborn calves
b. by stealth under the cover of a moonless night
c. as a means of negotiating a peace treaty between the two nations
d. they didn't, three Israelites stumbled upon it in a Philistine "garbage dump"

Why is Jesus taking so long in returning to earth?
a. He is patiently waiting so many people will repent and not be destroyed
b. He is carefully watching us to see who will live by faith
c. He is amusing himself by playing with our lives for as long as possible
d. He has actually forgotten about returning

Which Levite clan was assigned to carry all the tabernacle furnishings?
a. Korah   c. Merari
b. Gershon   d. Aaron

Who wrote the letter to Philemon?
- a. Peter
- c. James
- b. Paul
- d. John

(7)

What was King David's original occupation?
- a. slave
- c. tanner
- b. shepherd
- d. trader

(8)

Why did the dynamic divinely appointed team, Paul and Barnabas, split up?
- a. Barnabas was arrested
- b. Paul was arrested
- c. they could not agree about bringing the deserter John Mark with them
- d. God called Barnabas to go to Tarshish

(9)

How long did the flood waters cover earth?
- a. 40 days
- c. 365 days
- b. 150 days
- d. 515 days

(10)

SPARE:

Who said this: "Ye have brought us forth into this wilderness, to kill this whole assembly with hunger"?
- a. slaves under Nebuchadnezzar
- b. soldiers under David
- c. the crowd under Moses
- d. a mob under Pilate

Game 2 / Frame 7

HOW MANY PINS DID YOU KNOCK DOWN?

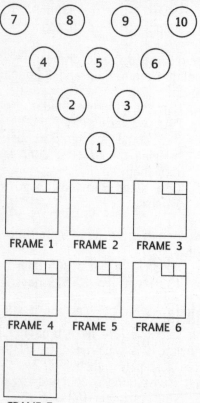

FRAME 1   FRAME 2   FRAME 3

FRAME 4   FRAME 5   FRAME 6

FRAME 7

Game 2/Frame 8

How did four friends of a paralyzed man get him through an overly crowded room to Jesus?
    a. they screamed "Romans" and created a panic to clear out the room
    b. they bribed people into leaving and never seeing Jesus again
    c. they ripped a hole in the roof and lowered the man in
    d. they knocked over two oil lamps and set the place on fire

What type of wood did God command Moses to build the ark of the covenant out of?
    a. oak   c. gopher
    b. acacia/shittim   d. cedar

How did the Israelites know for sure that the Egyptian army would never again threaten them?
    a. they saw the dead soldiers and horses washed up on the shore
    b. the invincible Edomites promised their "protection" on the Israel/Egypt border
    c. Pharaoh signed a peace treaty on papyrus scrolls
    d. God said so

What was King Saul's first big sin?
   a. he didn't want to fight a
       perceived losing battle as God
       commanded him to
   b. he didn't kill every breathing
       thing as God commanded him to
   c. he fought a battle that God
       neither commanded nor
       sanctioned
   d. he sacrificed burnt offerings
       instead of waiting for the
       prophet Samuel to do it

4

In the end-times, how many vials of
judgment will there be?
   a. 2   c. 7
   b. 5   d. 12

5

Which two gospels trace Jesus'
lineage through his earthly father,
Joseph?
   a. Matthew and Luke
   b. Luke and John
   c. Matthew and John
   d. Mark and Luke

6

What did the manna look like?
   a. yellow like honey wafers
   b. white like coriander seed
   c. brown like ripened wheat
   d. green like spring grass

7

Which one of Noah's sons tattled on his father's drunken state and nakedness?
- a. Shem
- b. Japheth
- c. Ham
- d. Cain

8

What Old Testament prophet's writings was the Ethiopian eunuch reading from but not understanding?
- a. Isaiah
- b. Jeremiah
- c. Moses
- d. Abraham

9

Who was the richest king on earth?
- a. Solomon
- b. David
- c. Josiah
- d. Ahab

10

SPARE:

Who said this: "Is thy God, whom thou servest continually, able to deliver thee"?
- a. Pharaoh of Egypt
- b. King Nebuchadnezzar of Babylon
- c. King Darius of Media/Persia
- d. Pontius Pilate of Rome

Game 2 / Frame 8

HOW MANY PINS
DID YOU KNOCK DOWN?

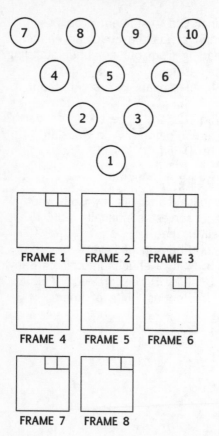

Game 2/Frame 9

Who tried to claim the throne while King David laid on his deathbed?
   a. his uncle, Joab
   b. his son, Adonijah
   c. his nephew, Barkiah
   d. his brother, Shammah

What was the name of the diseased beggar who died and went to Abraham's bosom?
   a. Lazarus   c. Caiaphas
   b. Nicodemus   d. Bartholomew

Which parable taught what it meant to be a good caring neighbor?
   a. the Pearl and the Pig
   b. the Fruitful Owner
   c. the Good Samaritan
   d. the Pharisee and the Publican

From what least likely spot did God bring forth water to quench the wandering Israelites?
   a. animal's skull
   b. dead tree
   c. tanned hide
   d. dusty rock

5

Which city's walls tumbled down at the sound of many trumpets and shouts?

a. Jerusalem   c. Jericho
b. Jordan   d. Jaez

What will ultimately happen to our earth and skies and everything belonging to them?

a. aliens will mine it until there are no more minerals, and we will die
b. it will all be set on fire and melt into nonexistence
c. we will keep evolving into better lives, until finally we will create heaven
d. it will never be destroyed because our technology will save it

6

What relationship existed between Aquila and Priscilla?

a. brother and sister
b. husband and wife
c. father and daughter
d. son and mother

7

Which Levite clan was assigned to carry the tabernacle basics like frames, posts, pegs, and ropes?

a. Kohath   c. Merari
b. Gershon   d. Aaron

8

What was King Saul's first battle at Jabesh-Gilead over?
- a. to save the inhabitants' right eyes from being thrust out by their enemies
- b. to save the inhabitants' right thumbs from being chopped off by their enemies
- c. to save the inhabitants' left ears from being lopped off by their enemies
- d. to save the inhabitants' front teeth from being knocked out by their enemies

How long did Jesus fast and resist Satan's temptations?
- a. 40 hours
- b. 40 days
- c. 40 weeks
- d. 40 months

SPARE:
Who said this: "How can a man be born when he is old? can he enter the second time into his mother's womb, and be born"?
- a. Samuel the prophet
- b. David the king
- c. Caiaphas the high priest
- d. Nicodemus the Pharisee

Game 2 / Frame 9

HOW MANY PINS DID YOU KNOCK DOWN?

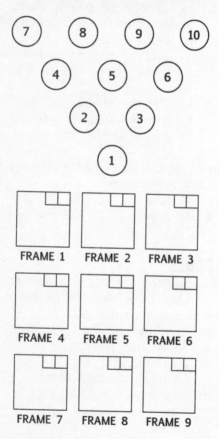

Game 2/Frame 10

What is the longest book in the Old Testament?
   a. Genesis
   b. Obadiah
   c. Psalms
   d. Jeremiah

What will happen to every single idle word spoken (that is, in a fit of temper, little white lies, etc.)?
   a. we will give an account on judgment day
   b. God will overlook them
   c. nothing, because no one is recording them
   d. our passage into heaven is based on the degree of idle words used

Zacharias was struck mute for unbelief. When did God allow him to speak again?
   a. after bathing in the Jordan river seven times
   b. after ten years of faithful service in the temple
   c. after declaring his baby son's name was John
   d. he never spoke again

How long did the very first human being live?
  a. 350 years   c. 930 years
  b. 640 years   d. 1,020 years

4

Which one of God's list of punishments did David choose as punishment for his unauthorized census?

5

  a. three years of famine
  b. three months fleeing from enemies
  c. three days of severe pestilence
  d. David could not bring himself to choose, so God chose one for him

What was Saul's original purpose for going to Damascus before he was converted?
  a. to check out how many people were still faithful Jews
  b. to visit his vacation spot

6

  c. he was lost due to the sudden windstorm God sent
  d. to harass and imprison every single Christian man or woman

Which son of King David sported very long thick hair?
  a. Abner

7

  b. Absalom
  c. Amnon
  d. Solomon

After Jesus rose from the dead, how much power did God give Him?
  a. all power on the earth
  b. all power in the heavens and on earth
  c. all power over spiritual unseen beings
  d. all power over material seen beings

What did James and John get their mother to ask Jesus for?
  a. for seats of highest prominence in the heavenly kingdom
  b. to bless them with faithful wives
  c. to be spared of the heartache of martyrdom
  d. forgiveness for their sins

Which of the following was never a judge of Israel?
  a. Gideon   c. Sisera
  b. Samson   d. Deborah

SPARE:

Who said this: "It is easier for a camel to go through the eye of a needle"?
  a. Peter   c. James
  b. Paul   d. Jesus

Game 2 / Frame 10

HOW MANY PINS
DID YOU KNOCK DOWN?

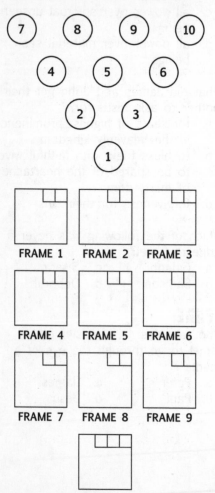

Game 2/Bonus Ball 1

Play only if you rolled a spare or strike in Frame 10.

Where was Moses buried?
a. on Mount Nebo under a pile of rocks
b. on Mount Sinai in the ground
c. he was carried into the Promised Land and buried there
d. nobody knows because God buried him

(1)

David was one of how many sons of Jesse?
a. 4
b. 8
c. 12
d. 16

(2)

Who received the Ten Commandments from God?
a. Adam
b. David
c. Moses
d. Solomon

(3)

Where was the temple tax, enough to pay for both Jesus and Peter, found?
a. in the dung of a camel that belonged to a passing nomad
b. in the mouth of a fish that Peter went out and caught
c. in the hem of a ruler's cloak
d. in the dirt beneath the third olive tree

(4)

5 What nation came from the incestuous relationship between Lot and his younger daughter?
   a. the Moabites
   b. the Hittites
   c. the Amorites
   d. the Ammonites

6 Who is Jesus, really?
   a. a prophet
   b. a good teacher
   c. a nice man
   d. the Son of God

7 What law of physics did Peter defy with Jesus' help?
   a. he walked on water
   b. he rose five feet in the air
   c. he shot electric sparks from his fingers
   d. he stepped into the midst of a raging fire

8 Who was brave enough to stay with Jesus after He was arrested?
   a. all twelve disciples
   b. only eleven disciples, because Judas had already committed suicide
   c. about half of them (Peter, James, John, Matthew, and Thomas)
   d. none of them

What common item did God use to allow Joshua and the Israelites to flatten Jericho's indestructible city walls?

9

a. shepherd's staff
b. an animal's jawbone
c. a ram's-horn trumpet
d. a smooth pebble

In the armor-of-God analogy, what did Paul liken the Word of God to?

a. sword   c. shoes   10
b. helmet   d. shield

SPARE:

Who said this: "We ought to obey God rather than men"?

a. Peter   c. James
b. Paul   d. John

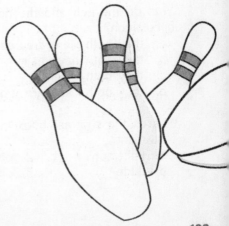

Game 2/Bonus Ball 2

Play only if you rolled strikes on Frame 10 and Bonus Ball 1.

1. Which river did God part for Joshua and the Israelites?
- a. Tigris
- b. Nile
- c. Jordan
- d. Euphrates

2. How old is God?
- a. 10 billion years old (He is older than the radiocarbon age of the earth)
- b. 2,044 years old (33 + 2,011)
- c. the scientific calculus-related formula takes eight steps to figure out
- d. He never had a beginning; He has always existed

3. What do the rich and the poor have in common?
- a. they both were created by God
- b. they both have hair
- c. they both laugh
- d. they both can earn money

4. What is the shortest book in the New Testament?
- a. Philemon
- b. Jude
- c. 2 John
- d. 3 John

Who said he was unworthy to touch the strap of Jesus' sandal?
- a. Herod the Great
- b. John the Baptist
- c. Caiaphas the high priest
- d. Felix the governor

5

Who penned the words to this psalm: "Against thee, thee only, have I sinned, and done this evil in thy sight"?
- a. David
- b. Moses
- c. the sons of Korah
- d. anonymous

6

Which of the following was not one of the five main cities of the Philistines?
- a. Ashdod   c. Gaza
- b. Ekron   d. Dagon

7

Which bird did Noah send out first to see if there was dry ground?
- a. pigeon   c. raven
- b. dove   d. owl

8

Golgotha means "the place of the skull" in which language?
- a. Greek
- b. Hebrew
- c. Aramaic
- d. Latin

9

What was the main reason why Paul left Titus in Crete?

a. to straighten out what was left unfinished and appoint elders in every town

b. to talk to the government leaders and get their support for the church

c. because they'd had an argument and Paul didn't want to see him

d. to tell the Cretan Christians that they had heretical ideas about Jesus

10

GAME 3

Game 3/Frame 1

What was the first miracle Jesus performed to show the world His glory?

    a. He made a man born blind see again

    b. He turned water into wine

    c. He ended a three-year drought with a huge rainstorm

    d. He called down fire from heaven

How rich was Jerusalem during King Solomon's reign?

    a. silver was so plentiful that it was as common as stones

    b. gold was so plentiful that it was as common as sand

    c. silk was so plentiful that it was used as common rags

    d. healing balms were so plentiful that even the lowest slave had excellent health

When Abraham and Lot parted ways, where did Lot and his family and his herds pitch their tents? Near:

    a. Haran   c. Sodom

    b. Ur   d. Gomorrah

Why did Jesus upset the money changers' tables as well as free the living sacrificial animals?
   a. they were selling rotten fruit and blemished animals
   b. they were conducting business on the Sabbath
   c. they were unruly and rebellious
   d. they were focused more on greedy haggling than on worshipping God

What lie did Abraham tell the Egyptian official regarding his wife, Sarah?
   a. she was his sister
   b. she was his mother
   c. she was his daughter
   d. she was his niece

What was the point to the parable of the rich fool?
   a. do not be so greedy
   b. store up treasure in heaven rather than amassing great wealth on earth
   c. how to acquire more gold for God
   d. what to do when servants complain

What is love?
- a. kissing and such
- b. romantic movies and books
- c. a warm fuzzy feeling
- d. God

How many apostles did Jesus have?
- a. 3
- b. 6
- c. 12
- d. 24

How many plagues did God inflict upon Egypt before Pharaoh let Moses and the Israelites go?
- a. 3
- b. 7
- c. 10
- d. 12

Who was the wife to King Ahab of Israel?
- a. Jezreel
- b. Jael
- c. Jezebel
- d. Jeri

SPARE:

Who said this: "Almost thou persuadest me to be a Christian"?
- a. Pontius Pilate
- b. Governor Felix
- c. Governor Festus
- d. King Agrippa

Game 3 / Frame 1

HOW MANY PINS
DID YOU KNOCK DOWN?

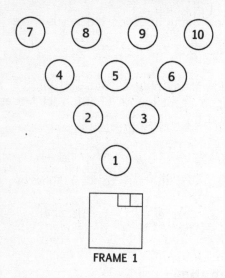

FRAME 1

Game 3/Frame 2

In the armor-of-God analogy, what should your feet be shod with?
- a. righteousness
- b. truth
- c. the gospel of peace
- d. love

1

What unusual thing did the soldiers accompanying Saul to Damascus see and hear?
- a. they saw nothing unusual but heard a voice
- b. they saw a strange man in glowing raiment but heard nothing
- c. they saw both a strange man in glowing raiment and heard a voice
- d. they did not see or hear anything unusual

2

What did the manna taste like?
- a. quail meat
- b. bitter herbs
- c. fruity mango
- d. honey wafers

3

What did Jonathan do that almost cost him his life?

   a. he took on the Philistines single-handedly

   b. he broke his father's oath of fasting and ate some honey

   c. he made love to a prostitute who bore him a son

   d. he stole money from the Lord's treasury to buy food

4

Who penned the words to this psalm: "O LORD, our Lord, how excellent is thy name in all the earth"?

5

   a. David

   b. Moses

   c. the sons of Korah

   d. anonymous

What country did little Jesus and his parents flee to after the wise men's visit?

   a. Egypt   c. Rome

   b. Syria   d. Babylon

6

Which evil queen devised a wicked plot to murder an innocent subject just to "legally" acquire his land?

7

   a. Esther   c. Jezebel

   b. Maacah   d. Athaliah

What was God's fatal punishment to the Israelites when they showed their unbelief ten times?
  a. every single person would die of starvation
  b. every adult was condemned to die in the wilderness
  c. every child would contract leprosy
  d. every child would die of thirst

8

From what city did Paul hail?
  a. Lystra   c. Cyprus
  b. Tarsus   d. Ephasus

9

What is it like to fall into the hands of the living God?
  a. fearful
  b. exciting and adventurous
  c. happy and joyful
  d. simple and worry free

10

SPARE:
Who said this: "As for me and my house, we will serve the LORD"?
  a. Joshua   c. Abraham
  b. Moses   d. Jacob

Game 3 / Frame 2

HOW MANY PINS
DID YOU KNOCK DOWN?

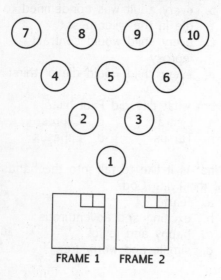

FRAME 1   FRAME 2

Game 3/Frame 3

What happened to the first ten spies who convinced Israel that trying to conquer the Promised Land was a hopeless battle?

a. they were struck dead with a plague

b. the earth opened up and swallowed them alive

c. they choked to death while eating quail

d. nothing because all of Israel were punished together via a plague

What monumental decision was made in the council at Jerusalem?

a. which apostles' gospels were to be canonized into the New Testament

b. which of the apostle Paul's many epistles were to be part of scripture

c. gentile converts must obey Moses' law like their Jewish counterparts

d. gentile converts were not to be burdened with every part of Moses' law

3 How many people did King Nebuchadnezzar throw into the fiery hot furnace?
   a. 1   c. 5
   b. 3   d. 7

4 Where did the Mary that Jesus cast seven demons out of come from?
   a. Ephesus   c. Magdala
   b. Corinth   d. Galilee

5 To God, what is a thousand years like?
   a. one minute
   b. one day
   c. a thousand days
   d. a thousand years

6 What was King Saul's second biggest sin?
   a. he didn't want to fight a perceived losing battle as God commanded him to
   b. he didn't kill every breathing thing as God commanded him to
   c. he fought a battle that God neither commanded nor sanctioned
   d. he sacrificed burnt offerings instead of waiting for the prophet Samuel to do it

What was Joseph to Jesus?
- a. His stepfather
- b. His biological father

7

- c. His stepbrother
- d. His biological brother

What did Lot's wife turn into when she looked back at the city she was fleeing for her life?

8

- a. stone
- b. salt
- c. lava
- d. fire

Throughout the Bible, what is the one word that is repeated three times to glorify God?

9

- a. Lord
- b. holy
- c. perfect
- d. righteous

How did King Saul die?
- a. he committed suicide
- b. he contracted leprosy

10

- c. he was murdered
- d. he died a natural death of old age

SPARE:

Who said this: "The spirit truly is ready, but the flesh is weak"?
- a. Moses
- b. Daniel
- c. Peter
- d. Jesus

Game 3 / Frame 3

HOW MANY PINS
DID YOU KNOCK DOWN?

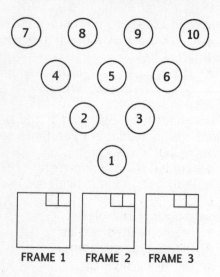

Game 3/Frame 4

What was the apostle Paul's original name?

1
   a. Samuel   c. Saul
   b. Seth   d. Simon

How do babies come about?
   a. by accident
   b. they evolve from apes
   c. by God's personal involvement 2
      inside every womb
   d. no one really knows for sure yet

What did the disciples find Jesus doing in the middle of a raging storm in the middle of the sea?

3
   a. sleeping   c. worrying
   b. praying   d. watching

Who penned the words to this psalm: "Be still, and know that I am God"?
   a. David
   b. Moses
   c. the sons of Korah   4
   d. anonymous

What tragedy befell Jacob's daughter, Dinah?
   a. she was born with only one arm

5
   b. she was raped by a foreigner
   c. she was murdered by a cousin
   d. she was mauled by a bear

What will not be present in the New Jerusalem?
- a. a temple, sun, and moon
- b. trees, birds, and animals
- c. technology, science, and math
- d. skyscrapers, houses, and stores

6

What did King Ahab use as a building material for his palace?

7

- a. gold   c. pearl
- b. silver   d. ivory

In the first year of the church era, how many people came to know Jesus as their personal Savior?
- a. about 100 people
- b. somewhere between 2,000 to 5,000 people
- c. over 8,000 people
- d. too many to accurately record

8

How many times can a person physically die?

9

- a. once
- b. depends on how well one lived this life
- c. about seven times
- d. perpetually, and be reincarnated

What was the reoccurring sin of the Israelites during the era of the Judges?

  a. everyone followed his own conscience instead of obeying God

  b. everyone offered blemished lamb sacrifices to God

  c. the priests were drunk and unruly most of the time

  d. the priests wanted land to inherit like all the other tribes

SPARE:

Who said this: "Am I my brother's keeper?"

  a. Abel   c. Esau

  b. Cain   d. Jacob

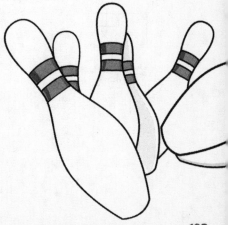

Game 3 / Frame 4

HOW MANY PINS DID YOU KNOCK DOWN?

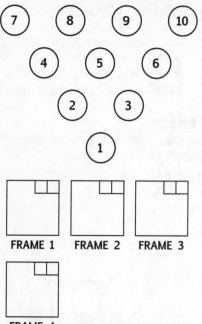

FRAME 1   FRAME 2   FRAME 3

FRAME 4

Game 3/Frame 5

What was Balaam's occupation?
1.
 a. god for hire
 b. prophet for hire
 c. king for hire
 d. servant for hire

Where did Jesus turn water into wine?
2.
 a. at the Passover
 b. at the Feast of Tabernacles
 c. at a funeral
 d. at a wedding

What kind of animals did Jesus permit some demons to possess?
3.
 a. cows   c. sheep
 b. pigs   d. goats

Who hid the two Israelites who were spying out Jericho?
4.
 a. Rahab   c. Roma
 b. Rebekah   d. Ruth

Which lesser-known prophet was a shepherd (or herdsman)?
5.
 a. Amos   c. Obadiah
 b. Nahum   d. Malachi

What was significant about the poor widow's offering of the two least-valuable coins?
  a. they were just found on the dusty ground outside; she sacrificed nothing to God
  b. they were two of the last ten coins she owned; she sacrificed a lot to God
  c. they were the last of her dowry inheritance; she sacrificed her nest egg to God
  d. they were the last two coins she owned in life; she sacrificed her all to God

6

On which day of creation did God create the oak tree?
  a. second   c. fourth
  b. third   d. fifth

7

What potentially fatal thing occurred during one of Paul's late-night preaching gigs?
  a. he was bitten by a viper
  b. a legion of Roman soldiers suddenly stormed the place
  c. a sleeping man fell from the third-floor window to the ground below
  d. a leprous man entered the crowded room

8

In the armor-of-God analogy, what does the shield represent?

9
a. righteousness c. truth
b. faith d. love

What was a former name of Jerusalem?

a. Palestine c. Jebusi
b. Salim d. Jetasebes

10

SPARE:

Who said this: "Let us go down, and there confound their language"?

a. Dagon c. Jesus
b. Balaam d. God

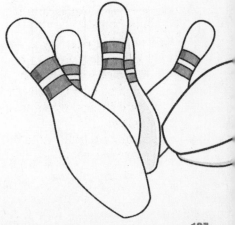

Game 3 / Frame 5

HOW MANY PINS DID YOU KNOCK DOWN?

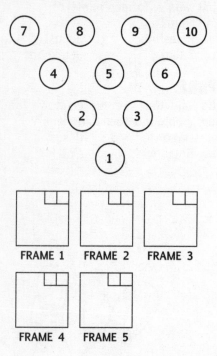

FRAME 1   FRAME 2   FRAME 3

FRAME 4   FRAME 5

Game 3/Frame 6

God commanded Noah to build an ark in preparation for which impending judgment?

1

- a. a worldwide dust storm
- b. a worldwide earthquake
- c. a worldwide flood
- d. a worldwide plague of locusts

What was the visible sign that the Holy Spirit entered into the disciples?

2

- a. they all had cloven tongues of fire above their heads
- b. they all started singing and dancing before the Lord
- c. all their hair became white as the prophet Moses' did after he had talked with God
- d. all their faces became bright as the prophet Moses' did after he had talked with God

What unusual thing did God command Hosea to do?

3

- a. marry a prostitute and have children
- b. eat only pigs and rabbits
- c. scatter human bones by the city gate
- d. make a fire for cooking, using dung as fuel

What did Elisha do upon deciding to heed the call to follow Elijah?
   a. asked for three months time so he could say good-bye to his family
   b. slaughtered his oxen and used the wooden yokes as firewood to roast his oxen
   c. ignored Elijah so Elijah had to use more forceful measures to convince him
   d. explained to Elijah that he needed a year's grace to close his business

4

What happened to Jesus after He was crucified?
   a. He didn't die, only fainted so the disciples nursed Him back to health
   b. He died, was buried, but the disciples stole his body and hid it
   c. He died, was buried, and rose again from the dead on the third day
   d. He was never crucified, only flogged and released

5

What famous person did Paul have to publicly confront regarding racial prejudice?
   a. James   c. Peter
   b. John   d. Timothy

6

What was the first of two methods God employed to decrease Gideon's army?

a. whoever was scared must depart
b. whoever lapped up water like a dog must depart
c. whoever wore his leather pouch over his right shoulder must depart
d. whoever was under five feet tall must depart

In the parable of the four soils, which soil represented the worldly cares and worries?

a. hard soil
b. weedy/thorny soil
c. thin layer of soil
d. good soil

What was Simon Peter's original occupation?

a. shepherd
b. fisherman
c. carpenter
d. tax collector

How did Jezebel die?

a. of old age
b. of a massive stroke followed by ten days of complete paralysis
c. she was assassinated by her son
d. she was thrown out of an upper window and trampled beneath horses' hooves

SPARE:

Who said this: "If I perish, I perish"?
a. Queen Esther
b. Queen Jezebel
c. King David
d. King Ahab

Game 3 / Frame 6

HOW MANY PINS
DID YOU KNOCK DOWN?

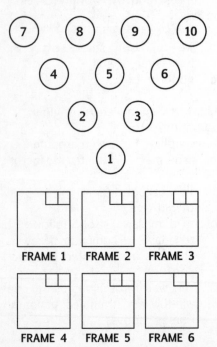

Game 3/Frame 7

1. Othniel, Israel's first judge, had a famous uncle. Who was he?
   a. Caleb
   b. Joshua
   c. Moses
   d. Judah

2. According to the Law, which of the following would be considered clean?
   a. rodents like weasels, ferrets, mice, and moles
   b. reptiles like lizards, geckos, tortoises, and chameleons
   c. they are all considered clean
   d. none of them are considered clean

3. How long did Jesus remain on earth after rising from the dead?
   a. 4 days
   b. 4 weeks
   c. 40 days
   d. 40 weeks

4. Who got swallowed up by a big fish and lived to talk about it?
   a. Joshua
   b. Jonah
   c. Jacob
   d. Jesus

5. Who were the two men who buried Jesus?
   a. Peter and John
   b. Annas and Caiaphas
   c. Joseph of Arimathaea and Nicodemus
   d. Judas and Matthew

What happened to Ananias and Sapphira when their lie was exposed?
a. they became lepers
b. they became paralyzed
c. they died
d. nothing, no one found out until much later

6

7

What was put on the stone that covered Jesus' burial spot?
a. a mini cross c. a seal
b. a banner d. a fish symbol

What did the Philistines put in the cart with the stolen ark of the covenant to appease God?
a. silver replicas of God's curses on them (mice and emerods)
b. gold replicas of God's curses on them (mice and emerods)
c. enough silver to weigh the equivalent of twelve cows
d. enough gold to weigh the equivalent of twelve cows

8

9

As the angel helped Peter escape from prison, how did the city gate open?
a. by itself
b. by a sleepwalking guard
c. by the angel
d. by an earthquake

What law of physics did God defy
when Joshua and the Israelites
battled against the Amorites?
  a. there was a midday eclipse
  b. it thundered when there were
      no clouds in the sky
  c. it snowed on the arid battlefield
  d. the sun stood still for one day

10

SPARE:

Who said this: "Eat, drink, and be
merry"?
  a. David after God helped them
      win a fierce battle
  b. the prostitute in a charge
      against her male "suitor"
  c. the publican/tax collector in a
      drunken state
  d. Jesus in a parable describing a
      rich fool

Game 3 / Frame 7

HOW MANY PINS DID YOU KNOCK DOWN?

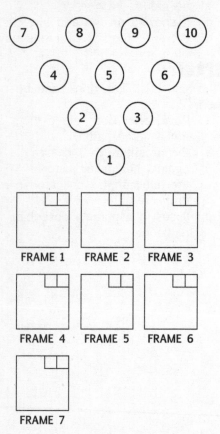

Game 3/Frame 8

1 At first, who did Mary think that Jesus was on Easter morning?
- a. soldier
- b. bystander
- c. mourner
- d. gardener

2 Who penned the words to this psalm: "Thy word is a lamp unto my feet, and a light unto my path"?
- a. David
- b. Moses
- c. the sons of Korah
- d. anonymous

3 Who was Eve's husband?
- a. Noah
- b. Adam
- c. Abraham
- d. Joseph

4 Which of the following did God not use as one of the ten plagues upon Egypt?
- a. boils
- b. leprosy
- c. hail
- d. frogs

5 What city did Timothy hail from?
- a. Lystra
- b. Tarsus
- c. Cyprus
- d. Ephesus

Why did Aquila and Priscilla leave Italy?
a. they got bored with the whole Roman culture
b. they had pressing lucrative business ventures in Greece
c. they were following a government order
d. they never really left Italy, only did lengthy vacations abroad

6

What was Nehemiah's original occupation?
a. governor over occupied Judah
b. cupbearer to a Persian king
c. arms bearer to the prophet Jeremiah
d. slave to an Assyrian king

7

What was the Jewish authorities' biggest problem with Jesus' teachings?
a. He kept claiming to be the Son of God
b. He kept making public spectacles out of them
c. He kept living a hypocritical lifestyle
d. He kept refusing to pay the temple tax

8

What is different about Samaria from all of the other cities and towns in Israel?
- a. it is the only city King Nebuchadnezzar could not defeat
- b. it is the only city that had no women in it due to its administrative function
- c. it is the only city built from the ground up, all of the rest were conquered
- d. it is the only city that had idols in the northern kingdom

Why did John not write down every single thing that Jesus did?
- a. he could not remember them all
- b. he did not feel they were significant enough
- c. he actually did but the second book has become lost over the years
- d. Jesus did so many things there were not enough books in the world to hold them all

SPARE:

Who said this: "Now lettest thou thy servant depart in peace, according to thy word: for mine eyes have seen thy salvation"?
- a. Simon
- b. Simeon
- c. James
- d. Jesus

Game 3 / Frame 8

HOW MANY PINS
DID YOU KNOCK DOWN?

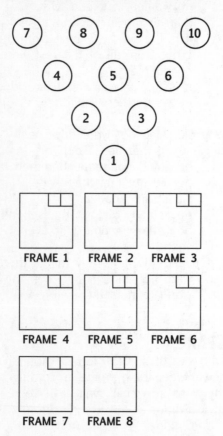

FRAME 1   FRAME 2   FRAME 3

FRAME 4   FRAME 5   FRAME 6

FRAME 7   FRAME 8

Game 3/Frame 9

What are the two longest books in the New Testament?

    a. Matthew and Acts
    b. Luke and Acts
    c. Romans and 1 Corinthians
    d. Luke and 1 Corinthians

What was baby Moses' basket made out of?

    a. grass and weeds
    b. bulrushes and pitch
    c. sticks and twigs
    d. straw and hay

When Jesus died and the earth quaked, whose bodies arose?

    a. no one   c. prophets
    b. kings   d. saints

What physical handicap did King Saul's grandson, Mephibosheth, have?

    a. he was blind
    b. he was deaf
    c. he was lame
    d. he was a midget

What occupation did Lydia have?
- a. none, she was the wife of a wealthy businessman
- b. dealer in purple cloth
- c. prostitute
- d. shepherdess

5

Who was sold into slavery by his brothers?
- a. Judah
- b. Levi
- c. Joseph
- d. Benjamin

6

How did King David die?
- a. he committed suicide
- b. he contracted leprosy
- c. he was murdered
- d. he died a natural death of old age

7

What was unusual about the hand that Jesus restored?
- a. it was withered
- b. it was paralyzed
- c. it was covered with leprosy
- d. it was chopped off

8

Who cried on Jesus' feet and wiped the tears off with hair?
- a. rich ruler
- b. penitent soldier
- c. remorseful disciple
- d. sinful woman

9

What dead body was carried with the Israelites when Pharaoh finally freed them?

a. Adam
b. Abraham
c. Noah
d. Joseph

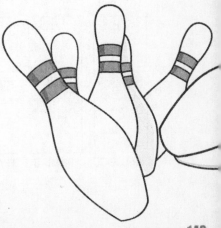

SPARE:

Who said this: "And now abideth faith, hope, charity, these three; but the greatest of these is charity"?

a. Peter
b. Paul
c. James
d. Jesus

Game 3 / Frame 9

HOW MANY PINS DID YOU KNOCK DOWN?

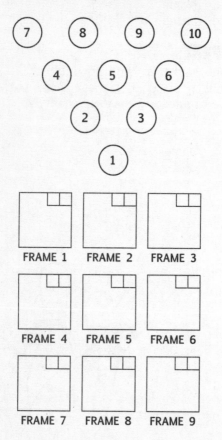

FRAME 1   FRAME 2   FRAME 3

FRAME 4   FRAME 5   FRAME 6

FRAME 7   FRAME 8   FRAME 9

Game 3/Frame 10

1 Who is the Holy Spirit?
   a. the believer's comforter and guarantee of God's promise
   b. a ghostly apparition
   c. the ruler over all angelic beings
   d. too mysterious to know for sure

2 What was Jesus' occupation before His public ministry?
   a. fisherman
   b. tax collector
   c. carpenter
   d. shepherd

3 In the armor-of-God analogy, what does the breastplate represent?
   a. righteousness   c. faith
   b. truth   d. gospel of peace

4 Who was Jacob's youngest son?
   a. Judah   c. Levi
   b. Dan   d. Benjamin

5 How was the Promised Land divided up between the tribes of Israel?
   a. by civil war and spoils
   b. by lots
   c. by the size of each tribe
   d. by preference

What was different about Elisha's hair that prompted bad children to jeer him?

   a. he was balding
   b. it was graying
   c. it was greasy
   d. it was lengthy

What was the second of two methods God employed to decrease Gideon's army?

   a. whoever was scared must depart
   b. whoever had not lapped up water like a dog must depart
   c. whoever wore his leather pouch over his right shoulder must depart
   d. whoever was under five feet tall must depart

How long had the prophetess Anna been a widow at the time Jesus was born?

   a. 84 days   c. 84 months
   b. 84 weeks   d. 84 years

Who was the first apostle to actually step into the empty tomb?

   a. Philip   c. James
   b. Peter   d. John

What were the people of Babel attempting to do?

- a. force God to show Himself on their terms
- b. turn their backs on God in disgust because of the evil He allowed to happen
- c. dig down to the center of the earth to hide from God
- d. build a tall tower to reach the heavens

SPARE:

Who said this: "It is finished"?

- a. Isaiah
- b. Jeremiah
- c. Jesus
- d. God

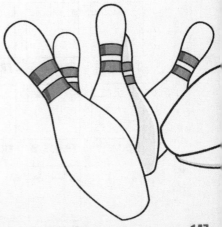

Game 3 / Frame 10

HOW MANY PINS DID YOU KNOCK DOWN?

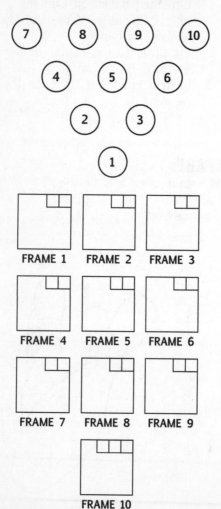

Game 3/Bonus Ball 1

Play only if you rolled a spare or strike in Frame 10.

1. What type of wood did Solomon build the Lord's temple out of?
   a. oak
   b. acacia
   c. gopher
   d. cedar

2. How were Jesus' burial clothes found in the empty tomb?
   a. dirty
   b. missing
   c. strewn about
   d. wrapped and folded neatly

3. What happened to the illegitimate son of King David and Bathsheba?
   a. he contracted leprosy
   b. he became blind
   c. he died
   d. nothing, but David contracted leprosy

4. During Israel's first battle in their national history, what did Moses do to help ensure victory?
   a. held his staff up in his hands
   b. stood on one foot
   c. conducted the Levite choir in loudly praising God
   d. prayed continually in the tabernacle of God

5. Who was the last ruling king in the southern kingdom of Judah before Babylon overtook it?
   a. Jeroboam
   b. Jehoiachin
   c. Hoshea
   d. Zedekiah

6. How many pieces of silver did Judas betray Jesus for?
   a. 3
   b. 30
   c. 300
   d. 3000

7. Who was Onesimus?
   a. responsible slave owner
   b. runaway slave
   c. AWOL soldier
   d. harsh centurion

8. On what day were the disciples filled with the Holy Spirit?
   a. Easter
   b. Passover
   c. Pentecost
   d. Yom Kippur

9. What common item did God use to cure Naaman of his leprosy?
   a. dirty river
   b. obscure mountain
   c. shepherd's staff
   d. prostitute's outer raiment

What incident occurred between the twelve-year-old Jesus and His parents?

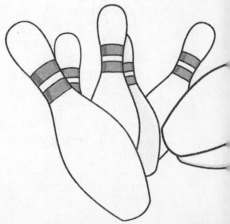

a. some boys beat Him for his "righteous" speeches
b. He was tempted by Satan with a pretty girl his age
c. He was still in Jerusalem after His parents had started heading for home
d. He banged his thumb with a hammer in his father's carpenter shop

SPARE:

Who said: "Let there be light"?

a. Isaiah   c. Jesus
b. Jeremiah   d. God

Game 3/Bonus Ball 2

Play only if you rolled strikes on Frame 10 and Bonus Ball 1.

What was unusual about Peter's dream with the sheet dropping down out of the sky?

   a. a voice commanded him to eat the unclean pig on the sheet
   b. a voice commanded him to eat only the unclean fish on the sheet
   c. a voice commanded him to eat the unclean fowl on the sheet
   d. a voice commanded him to eat all the unclean creatures on the sheet

What was unusual about Jacob's great-granddaughter-in-law's twins? Under Jewish law:

   a. their biological father was actually their grandfather, Jacob's son
   b. their biological father was actually their great-uncle, Jacob's brother
   c. their biological mother was actually their great-aunt, Jacob's sister
   d. their biological mother was actually a Canaanite prostitute

What was the only sign Jesus promised to give the unbelieving crowd when they demanded proof of His deity?

3

    a. the sign of Jonas
    b. the sign of Elijah
    c. the sign of Abraham
    d. the sign of Moses

Who penned the words to this psalm: "The LORD is my shepherd; I shall not want"?

    a. David
    b. Moses
    c. the sons of Korah
    d. anonymous

4

What did God part for Moses and the Israelites after they left Egypt?

5

    a. the clouds   c. the sea
    b. the river   d. the desert

Who are the only five women listed in Jesus' genealogy?

    a. Sarah, Rebekah, Ruth, Hannah, Mary
    b. Rebekah, Leah, Miriam, Deborah, Mary
    c. Eve, Rachel, Hannah, Esther, Mary
    d. Tamar, Rahab, Ruth, Bathsheba, Mary

6

What request did Elijah make of the starving widow during the lengthy famine?

a. do no work for three days as on a Sabbath and then look in your storage vessels

b. make rows in dirt as if plowing seeds and look for sprouts the next morning

c. prepare the last batch of bread and give me the first portion of it

d. borrow as many jars as possible and watch as God fills them with oil

7

What did Gideon's father call him after Gideon tore down the city's altar to Baal?

a. Jezebel   c. Jonathan
b. Jerubbaal   d. Jerkabaal

8

Who was the mother of John the Baptist?

a. Mary   c. Elizabeth
b. Miriam   d. Lydia

9

What did Paul ask Philemon for when he would visit him?

a. lodging
b. a meal
c. a set of writing tools
d. a new cloak

10

GAME 4

Game 4/Frame 1

1. Which chapter in Proverbs beautifully illustrates what the ideal godly wife should be?
   a. 1
   b. 23
   c. 31
   d. 54

2. What happened to King Sihon when he mobilized his army against Moses and the Israelites?
   a. complete slaughter and annihilation
   b. complete slavery for the next three generations
   c. partial slaughter (fighting army men) and partial slavery (woman and children)
   d. partial slaughter and partial slavery (indiscriminate for both)

3. What was Abraham's original name?
   a. Abraham
   b. Abram
   c. Abe
   d. Abramson

4. How many other criminals were crucified with Jesus?
   a. none
   b. one
   c. two
   d. three

Which Old Testament prophet tended sycamore fruit trees?

5

   a. Amos   c. Micah
   b. Obadiah   d. Nahum

According to the Law, which of the following would be considered clean?

   a. ants and locusts
   b. spiders and locusts
   c. worms and locusts
   d. grasshoppers and locusts

6

Why did Jesus speak in parables so often?

7

   a. He was gifted in telling short stories
   b. to hide God's wisdom from those who chose to disbelieve
   c. it was a pleasant alternative to John the Baptist's harsh teachings
   d. the crowd kept asking for yet one more parable

In the parable of the four soils, which soil represented faith that has no substance?

   a. hard soil
   b. weedy/thorny soil
   c. stony soil
   d. good soil

8

Where did the antagonists accuse
Jesus of getting His power to
exorcise from?
- a. Baal, god of the Canaanites
- b. Beelzebub, prince of devils
- c. Zeus, top god of the Greeks
- d. Apollo, top god of the Romans

How many sons did Leah bear
Jacob?
- a. 2   c. 6
- b. 3   d. 12

SPARE:

Who said this: "This do in
remembrance of me"?
- a. Joshua   c. David
- b. Jesus   d. Peter

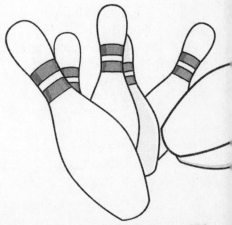

Game 4 / Frame 1

HOW MANY PINS DID YOU KNOCK DOWN?

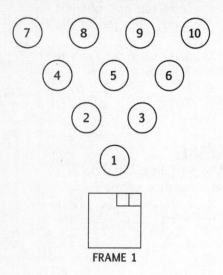

FRAME 1

Game 4/Frame 2

1. What was the answer to Hannah's prayer?
- a. a husband
- b. a son
- c. a job
- d. a meal

2. Who was the only person who lived before the flood and did not die?
- a. Esau
- b. Enoch
- c. Elisha
- d. Elijah

3. Who was Jacob's brother?
- a. Abel
- b. Lot
- c. Isaac
- d. Esau

4. For all the pent-up hatred the Jewish rulers had toward Jesus, what was the most difficult part of His night trial?
- a. He kept miraculously escaping their clutches, both in speech and in action
- b. He kept redirecting the questions back to them and their sin
- c. they could not get two false witnesses to accuse Him of the same "crime"
- d. they could not figure out how to get Him to obey them

When did God part the Jordan river en route to Jericho?

a. after all the feet of the priests carrying the ark of the Lord were in the river

b. at dusk, just after the evening sacrifices were made

c. immediately after commanding the Israelites to prepare for battle

d. it was the sea that God parted, not the river

In the wheat and tares parable, what does the wheat represent?

a. the world

b. the children of the kingdom

c. the children of the wicked one

d. the Son of Man

Of what ethnicity was Timothy?

a. Roman/Greek

b. African/Jewish

c. Greek/African

d. Jewish/Greek

Who was the prophet-priest in forced exile?

a. Isaiah in Assyria

b. Jonah in Nineveh

c. Jeremiah in Babylon

d. Ezekiel in Babylon

How did the five kings hide when they were trying to escape from Joshua and the Israelites?

9

   a. they disguised themselves as peasants
   b. they hid in a cave
   c. they fled across the wilderness to Egypt
   d. they fled across the desert to Ur

When will Jesus return?

   a. in about three more generations
   b. after we humans know everything there is to know
   c. before the third millennium arrives
   d. no one knows except God the Father

10

SPARE:

Who said this: "Here am I; send me"?

   a. Isaiah
   b. Jeremiah
   c. Jesus
   d. Paul

Game 4 / Frame 2

HOW MANY PINS DID YOU KNOCK DOWN?

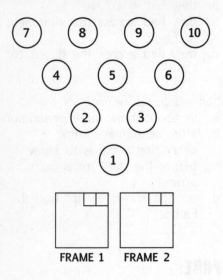

FRAME 1   FRAME 2

Game 4/Frame 3

What is real charity/love?
   a. popularity and wealth
   b. sex within marriage
   c. godly characteristics
   d. there is no such thing as real love

What was John commanded to do with the little book the angel gave him?
   a. bury it   c. eat it
   b. hide it   d. ignore it

Which king ordered the slaughter of a priest and his whole family for the supposed crime of treason?
   a. Saul   c. Solomon
   b. David   d. Ahab

What did the Shunammite woman's son suddenly start screaming about while he was out in the fields?
   a. Ammonite raiders were racing toward them
   b. a swarm of locusts were flying toward them
   c. he accidentally chopped off his hand with the sickle
   d. he had a massively painful headache

After Paul and Barnabas's first visit to Lystra, who did the people think Paul was?

5

a. Mars /Ares
b. Jupiter/Zeus
c. Mercurius/Hermes
d. Sol/Apollo

Who penned the words of this psalm: "Make a joyful noise unto to the LORD, all ye lands"?

a. David
b. Moses
c. the sons of Korah
d. anonymous

6

What was the point to the parable of the prodigal son?

7

a. God seeks the backsliders, the "sinners," according to society, so they can repent and enter heaven
b. God wants everyone to live perfectly like the older son
c. God enters into communion with those who finally become holy
d. God has the "warm fuzzies" for all his creatures

What did God command Ezekiel to
use for fuel to cook his meals?
  a. cow dung
  b. human flesh
  c. rotting animals
  d. donkey jawbones

8

What is something that a lazy man
says as a flimsy excuse to not work?
  a. there is a lion out there and I'll
     get eaten
  b. there is an elephant at the door
     and I'll get trampled
  c. there is hail on the streets and
     I'll get wounded
  d. there is flooding at my
     neighbor's house and I'll drown

9

Which prophet was taken up in a
chariot of fire?
  a. Elijah   c. Ezekiel
  b. Elisha   d. Daniel

10

SPARE:
Who said this: "Naked came I out of
my mother's womb, and naked shall I
return thither"?
  a. David   c. Job
  b. Daniel   d. Jesus

Game 4 / Frame 3

HOW MANY PINS DID YOU KNOCK DOWN?

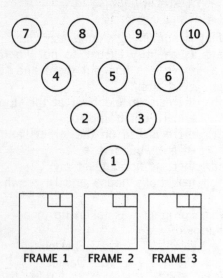

FRAME 1   FRAME 2   FRAME 3

Game 4/Frame 4

What happened to the huge Philistine god Dagon during the second night after the Philistines captured Israel's ark of the covenant?

1

   a. it howled eerily like a wounded jackal

   b. it turned sooty black except for its feet

   c. it fell down, breaking off its head and hands

   d. nothing, it was the Philistines who died mysteriously during the night

What did God change Jacob's name to?

   a. Sidon   c. Nimrod

   b. Israel   d. Babylon

2

3

What shape will the New Jerusalem's city be?

   a. square   c. circle

   b. rectangle d. triangle

Which bird did Noah send out that returned with an olive leaf in her beak?

   a. pigeon   c. crow

   b. dove   d. sparrow

4

What did the Jerusalem mob assume
Paul had done that led to his arrest?
  a. murdered a fellow human being
  b. eaten bacon and wine
  c. polluted the Lord's temple by
     letting Greek gentiles in
  d. healed on the Sabbath

After Nabal refused to help David,
who had protected his land during
war, how did God punish Nabal?
  a. he had a stroke and was totally
     paralyzed for ten days before
     finally dying
  b. Chaldean raiders came and
     burned down his house
  c. Amorite soldiers slaughtered all
     his animals
  d. he contracted leprosy and
     suffered for the rest of his
     shortened life

What occurred in the valley in
Ezekiel's vision?
  a. a few raindrops turned into
     flood waters
  b. many enemy soldiers suddenly
     fell down dead for no reason
  c. hundreds of four-footed beasts
     stampeded Babylon
  d. thousands of scattered skeleton
     bones rattled to life

When the angel helped Peter escape from prison, how did the praying Jews receive him?
 a. with disbelief
 b. with anger
 c. with both
 d. with neither

What is down the middle of New Jerusalem's "Main Street"?
 a. the trees of life
 b. the river of the water of life
 c. people worshipping God
 d. people praying to God

Besides King Solomon and Lemuel, who else wrote Proverbs?
 a. Agur   c. Abraham
 b. Amos   d. Assuer

SPARE:

Who said this: "For unto you is born this day in the city of David a Saviour, which is Christ the Lord"?
 a. God   c. a prophet
 b. an angel   d. a shepherd

Game 4 / Frame 4

HOW MANY PINS
DID YOU KNOCK DOWN?

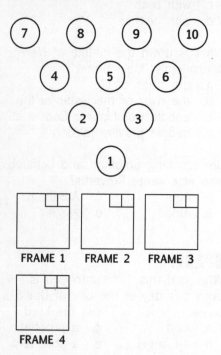

FRAME 1   FRAME 2   FRAME 3

FRAME 4

Game 4/Frame 5

What did disloyal Shimei do to King David and his men while they were on the run?

1

    a. he cursed them while pelting them with stones

    b. he spit in their faces

    c. he spread maliciously false rumors about them

    d. he bribed bad men to continually attack and harass them

Who was thrown into the den of lions?

2

    a. David   c. Demetrius

    b. Daniel   d. Delilah

When the Jewish exiles returned home and started to rebuild the temple, what did their nearby neighbors do?

3

    a. helped them with supplies and labor

    b. gave them their cedar trees for a low price

    c. raided their camp for many months

    d. frustrated every effort through a nasty letter-writing campaign

How many epistles did Paul write to Titus?

- a. 0
- b. 1
- c. 2
- d. 3

4

In the New Jerusalem, what purpose do the leaves on the trees of life serve?

5

- a. purely aesthetic purposes
- b. they exchange the carbon dioxide in the air for clean air
- c. they provide necessary nourishment to the heavenly inhabitants
- d. they heal the nations

How many provinces did Queen Esther's husband rule over?

- a. 52
- b. 127
- c. 368
- d. 575

6

What was King Saul's chief reason for hating David?

7

- a. revenge
- b. jealousy
- c. rivalry
- d. anger

What miraculously filled all the poor widow's many borrowed jars?

- a. gold
- b. coins
- c. oil
- d. flour

8

How did Moses destroy the golden calf?
   a. he broke it up into many pieces and buried them deep in the earth
   b. he burned it, crushed it, mixed it with water, and forced the Israelites to drink it
   c. he saved it as an example of supreme disobedience to the Lord God Almighty
   d. he melted it down and used the gold for holy articles in the tabernacle

What does the name *Barnabas* mean?
   a. "son of thunder/noise"
   b. "son of consolation/encouragement"
   c. "son of happiness/joyful"
   d. "son of sorrow/sadness"

SPARE:

Who said this: "Nevertheless not my will, but thine, be done"?
   a. Isaiah   c. Jesus
   b. Jeremiah   d. Paul

Game 4 / Frame 5

HOW MANY PINS DID YOU KNOCK DOWN?

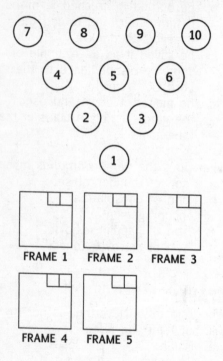

Game 4/Frame 6

How did God provide for Elijah's needs when the prophet fled from Queen Jezebel's lethal rage?
- a. twice an angel gave him warm bread and a jar of water in the middle of nowhere
- b. once a camel came bearing new clothes
- c. three times a friend came to encourage him
- d. two different strangers offered their homes to Elijah the political refugee

What happened to the place of prayer when the early church praised God after Peter and John were released after they were brought before the Jewish council?
- a. the place caught on fire
- b. the place was flooded
- c. the place was shaken
- d. the place was buffeted by mighty winds

Which prophet delivered God's message of assured victory over Assyria's strong army and the king's insulting chief of staff?
- a. Isaiah
- b. Jeremiah
- c. Ezekiel
- d. Daniel

After entering the Promised Land, in which city did Israel set up the tabernacle?

a. Shiloh   c. Gibash
b. Bethlehem   d. Jerusalem

4

What type of wood did God command Noah to build the ark out of?

5

a. oak   c. gopher
b. acacia   d. cedar

When Jesus rested for a short time at Jacob's well, whom did He chat with?

a. a shepherd who used to be that area's tax collector
b. a woman who had five husbands and currently slept with yet another man
c. a rich ruler from Ethiopia
d. a beggar who was extremely inquisitive regarding spiritual matters

6

Who warned Pilate not to get involved with Jesus' trial?

a. his top advisor because of fortune-telling omens
b. his son because of a rumor he heard circulating among the soldiers
c. his wife because of a troubling dream she had
d. his foreign cupbearer because of an ancient legend regarding a "holy one"

7

On which day of creation did God create Adam?

- a. fourth
- b. fifth
- c. sixth
- d. seventh

8

What mistake did Jacob purposely commit when blessing two of his grandchildren?

9

- a. called them by two of their uncles' names (Judah and Levi)
- b. gave them an Egyptian blessing instead of a Hebrew one
- c. gave the younger one the bigger blessing reserved for the firstborn
- d. called the younger one by his brother's name and vice versa

In the parable of the four soils, which soil represented spiritual growth and maturity?

- a. hard soil
- b. weedy/thorny soil
- c. thin layer of soil
- d. good soil

10

SPARE:

Who said this: "Woe unto them that call evil good, and good evil"?

- a. God via Isaiah
- b. God via Jeremiah
- c. God via Jesus
- d. God via Paul

Game 4 / Frame 6

HOW MANY PINS DID YOU KNOCK DOWN?

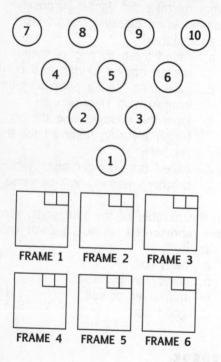

Game 4/Frame 7

1. What was the name of Bathsheba's murdered husband?
   a. Uriah
   b. Jehoiah
   c. Baalzebub
   d. David

2. How will God destroy His enemies in the absolute final battle on earth?
   a. flood the world with the waters of the sea
   b. devour them with fire from the heavens
   c. annihilate the world with the gases of the sun going supernova
   d. eradicate the world with technological "beings" from space

3. In Proverbs, how is wisdom portrayed?
   a. a talking lamb
   b. a talking owl
   c. a woman pleading in the streets for people to follow her ways
   d. a man shouting from the hilltop

4. For whom did the crowd scream to be released during the annual Passover tradition?
   a. Barnabas
   b. Barabbas
   c. Bartholomew
   d. Benjamin

What clever plot did King David use to murder Uriah?

a. he ordered that Uriah be arrested on charges of treason and "lawfully" executed
b. he ordered Uriah to be on the battlefront and have the enemy "militarily" kill him
c. he arranged for Uriah to have a fatal "accident" while traveling back to the army
d. he arranged for a prostitute to lure Uriah into a wine-induced death

What did David do in the presence of a fearsome Philistine king?

a. fell at the king's feet and begged for mercy
b. betrayed Israel by giving out two minor military battle plans
c. spoke in a rare foreign language so no one would understand him
d. acted mad, drooling down his beard and scratching on the city gate

What was Barnabas's original name?

a. Joshua   c. Jacob
b. John   d. Joses

Who brought food to Elijah while he camped out at Kerith Brook during the famine?
  a. his faithful servant, Rael-beson
  b. a nearby king, Pajubinto
  c. ravens
  d. donkeys

(8)

In the wheat and tares parable, what do the tares represent?
  a. the world
  b. children of the kingdom
  c. children of the wicked one
  d. devil/Satan

(9)

Who penned the words to this psalm: "As far as the east is from the west, so far hath he removed our transgressions from us"?
  a. David
  b. Moses
  c. the sons of Korah
  d. anonymous

(10)

SPARE:
Who said this: "My God, my God, why hast thou forsaken me?"
  a. Abraham   c. Jesus
  b. Moses   d. Paul

Game 4 / Frame 7

HOW MANY PINS
DID YOU KNOCK DOWN?

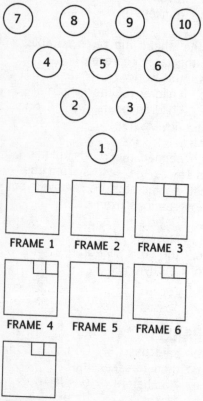

Game 4/Frame 8

1. What type of metal overlaid the wood altar in the Lord's tabernacle?
- a. gold
- b. silver
- c. brass
- d. tin

2. Where was Jesus born?
- a. Galilee
- b. Nazareth
- c. Bethlehem
- d. Jerusalem

3. How did the brothers react when Joseph revealed himself as the one they sold into slavery?
- a. troubled and terrified
- b. angry and full of curses
- c. awed and humbled
- d. glad and relieved

4. What will Satan do as soon as he is released from his prison?
- a. fall at God's feet and beg for mercy
- b. deceive as many people as possible to side with him in the final battle
- c. hatch a plan to assassinate God
- d. try to escape God's clutches by hiding in the most remote part of space

Where did the prophet Samuel grow up?

5
- a. in the tabernacle
- b. in the temple
- c. at home
- d. in the house of houses

On the day of Pentecost, what sound announced the arrival of the Holy Spirit?

- a. still small whisper
- b. bleating sheep
- c. falling water
- d. rushing mighty winds

6

What type of bird meat did God provide for the Israelites in the wilderness?

7
- a. dove
- b. raven
- c. quail
- d. ostrich

What was the name of Queen Esther's predecessor?

- a. Vasi
- b. Vashti
- c. Venus
- d. Veronica

8

After Paul and Barnabas's first visit to Lystra, who did the people think Barnabas was?

9
- a. Mars/Ares
- b. Jupiter/Zeus
- c. Mercurius/Hermes
- d. Sol/Apollo

According to the Law, which of the following would be considered clean?

a. eagle
b. owl
c. pigeon
d. stork

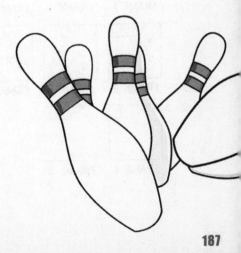

SPARE:

Who said this: "I have planted, Apollos watered; but God gave the increase"?

a. Peter
b. Paul
c. James
d. Jesus

Game 4 / Frame 8

HOW MANY PINS DID YOU KNOCK DOWN?

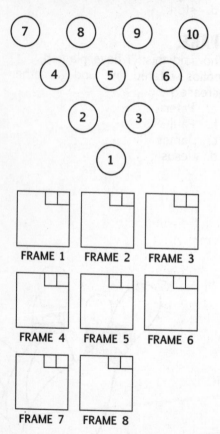

Game 4/Frame 9

What fatal sin did Aaron's sons Nadab and Abihu commit?

a. they wrongly offered fire to God
b. they offered the wrong kind of animal to God
c. they ate the tabernacle's bread while the high priest Aaron was still alive
d. they ate the fat from the lamb offered to God

How many books are in the Old Testament?

a. 27   c. 52
b. 39   d. 66

What was unusual about Ehud, Israel's second judge?

a. he was a midget
b. he was a giant
c. he was left-handed
d. he was a foreigner

As part of the Roman soldiers' torture, what did they force on to Jesus' head?

a. helmet of nails
b. crown of thorns
c. hood of pigskins
d. bag of broken bones

What finally convinced the crowd that the disciples were filled with the Holy Spirit and not drunk on Pentecost?

5

    a. it was too early in the morning to be drunk
    b. the crowd understood the disciples' "babbling" as their own native languages
    c. all of the above
    d. none of the above

What did God command Joshua and the men to do to memorialize God's miracle of parting the Jordan River?

6

    a. take twelve stones from the middle of the river and set them up on the shore
    b. place the ram horns used in the miracle into the ark of the Lord
    c. chisel the miracle narrative into a huge rock
    d. take off their shoes and walk barefoot for three days

What did the little book that the angel gave John to eat taste like?

7

    a. sweet, then bitter
    b. salty, then sweet
    c. fruity, then salty
    d. sour, then fruity

How many sons did Rachel's handmaiden, Bilhah, bear Jacob?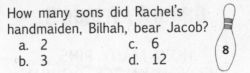
- a. 2
- b. 3
- c. 6
- d. 12

What did God say after Moses destroyed the first set of divinely inscribed stone tablets in a fit of temper?
- a. you blew it, and I won't bother showing you people mercy anymore
- b. chisel out two more stone tablets, and I'll rewrite my laws onto them
- c. I'll rewrite them, but I'm going to add a few more because you people are bad
- d. give me one reason why I shouldn't just kill you all off right here and now

Who replaced the dead traitor, Judas Iscariot, to be counted as the twelfth apostle?
- a. Joseph
- b. Barabbas
- c. Justus
- d. Matthias

SPARE:

Who said this: "The cock shall not crow, till thou hast denied me thrice"?
- a. Peter
- b. Paul
- c. James
- d. Jesus

Game 4 / Frame 9

HOW MANY PINS DID YOU KNOCK DOWN?

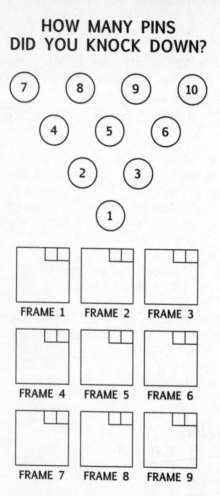

Game 4/Frame 10

What did Eli the priest assume was Hannah's problem when he saw her lying on the ground with her lips silently moving?

a. she was drunk, so he rebuked her

b. she was mugged, so he helped her

c. she was ill, so he let her lodge near the tabernacle

d. she was in deep prayer, so he left her alone

What is another name for Esau?

a. Onam

b. Shobal

c. Haran

d. Edom

What was one of main purposes of the cities of refuge in the Promised Land?

a. a woman who was divorced could live there in safety

b. a woman who was widowed could live there and have her basic needs provided for

c. a man guilty of stealing could live there and not suffer the horrid punishment

d. a man guilty of accidental murder could live there without threats to his life

How old was the man who had been crippled since birth, when Peter and John healed him?
a. a teenager
b. over 30 years old
c. over 40 years old
d. over 60 years old

4

How will Jesus return to earth?
a. as a humble servant
b. on a lightning bolt
c. on a donkey
d. in the same way He left it

5

Who penned the words to this psalm: "Teach us to number our days, that we may apply our hearts unto wisdom"?
a. David
b. Moses
c. the sons of Korah
d. anonymous

6

As believers in Jesus, how should we act?
a. point out other people's errors
b. be so meek as to let others walk all over us
c. be quick to listen, slow to speak, slow to be angry
d. wave the Bible in other people's faces

7

Who was the father of John the Baptist?
- a. Zacharias
- c. Joseph
- b. Matthew
- d. Philip

8

What was Moses' father-in-law's wise advice?
- a. create a second set of priests so God is praised 24-7
- b. create another copy of the Ten Commandments just in case
- c. appoint men to help judge so you avoid job-related burnout
- d. appoint one day every week for rest to avoid exhaustion

9

What article of clothing did Jacob give to his favorite son, Joseph?
- a. sandals made of camel hides
- b. a turban made of newly discovered silks
- c. a coat made of many colors
- d. a cloak made of many animal skins

10

SPARE:

Who said this: "Speak; for thy servant heareth"?
- a. Samuel
- c. Paul
- b. Saul
- d. Jesus

Game 4 / Frame 10

HOW MANY PINS DID YOU KNOCK DOWN?

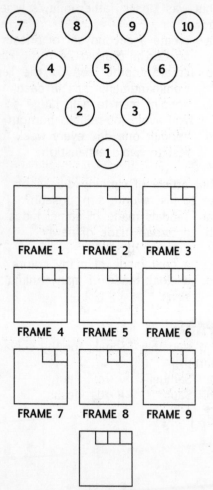

Game 4/Bonus Ball 1

Play only if you rolled a spare or strike in Frame 10.

What does *Kibrothhattaavah* mean?
a. graves of gluttony because the Israelites lusted for and gorged themselves on quail
b. field of snakes because of the biting vipers
c. rock of refuge because God protected Israel from the Hittite army
d. sky of gladness because Israel received much-needed rainfall

What were the two things God absolutely forbade anyone from eating on a dead animal?
a. skin and fat
b. fat and blood
c. blood and bones
d. bones and skin

Who did God appoint to go with Saul during his first missionary trip?
a. Silas
b. Barnabas
c. John
d. Timothy

What did God create as a sign of His promise to never flood the whole earth again?

a. olive trees   c. a rainbow
b. starry skies   d. doves

4

In the seven letters to the seven churches, which church had lost its first love?

5
a. Sardis   c. Pergamos
b. Smyrna   d. Ephesus

What military strategy did God command Joshua and the army to deploy against Ai?

a. ambush
b. full charge
c. circle their camp seven times while blowing trumpets
d. do nothing and believe that God will plague the enemy during the night

6

How did God punish Korah and his 250 rebels who dared to presume they were just as qualified to be priests as Aaron?

7
a. poisoned them with snake venom
b. drowned them from the flooded riverbanks
c. opened up the earth and swallowed them
d. burned them to a crisp from fire coming from the Lord Himself

In the parable of the four soils, which soil represented the people who refuse to believe?

a. hard soil by the wayside
b. weedy/thorny soil
c. thin layer of soil
d. good soil

8

How many sons did Rachel bear Jacob?

9

a. 2   c. 6
b. 3   d. 12

How did John the Baptist describe himself when interrogated by the Jewish authorities?

a. the voice of God
b. the voice of reason
c. the voice of one crying in the wilderness
d. the voice of one yelling on the street corner

10

SPARE:

Who said this: "Man shall not live by bread alone"?

a. Paul quoting David
b. Job quoting Abraham
c. Esther quoting Ruth
d. Jesus quoting Moses

Game 4/Bonus Ball 2

Play only if you rolled strikes on Frame 10 and Bonus Ball 1.

Who were the only Jericho residents to survive the defeat of their city?
  a. no one, God commanded every single living thing to die
  b. all women and girls who had never borne a child
  c. the king and his top aides
  d. Rahab and her family under her roof

Why was the book of Lamentations written?
  a. Jeremiah mourned the fall of Zion and its people becoming slaves
  b. David mourned the death of his best friend, Jonathan
  c. Lot mourned for his wife who was turned into a pillar of salt
  d. the apostles mourned the death of Jesus, the Son of God

What was Sarah's original name?
  a. Sarah
  b. Sara
  c. Sarai
  d. Sari

In the crowd of over 5,000 people, who found the boy with the fish and bread lunch?
   a. a prostitute Jesus just forgave of her sins
   b. Andrew, the apostle to Jesus
   c. a soldier who had come to test Jesus
   d. a Pharisee

4

What happens to the scapegoat after a year's worth of sins have been prayerfully transferred to his head?
   a. it is released into the wilderness
   b. it is sacrificed on the Lord's altar
   c. it is mated with the previous year's scapegoat to represent ongoing sin
   d. it is slaughtered and burned outside of the Israelite camp

5

How did Judas betray Jesus?
   a. hug
   b. kiss
   c. bow
   d. smile

6

Who did God appoint as the very first high priest in Jewish history?
   a. Moses   c. Eli
   b. Aaron   d. Samuel

7

What concern did the five daughters of Zelophehad bring to Moses?

a. who would marry them since they were condemned prostitutes
b. who would take care of them since they were orphans
c. who would inherit their father's land since they had no brothers
d. who would care for their children since they contracted leprosy

What is so important about the Word of God?

a. the Word was what prophets used to confront the kings
b. the Word was an interesting work of fiction mixed with facts
c. the Word was to be used as a supplement to moral teachings
d. the Word was God and with God since before the beginning of time

In the seven letters to the seven churches, which church was found lukewarm?

a. Laodicea   c. Pergamos
b. Smyrna   d. Ephesus

ANSWERS

GAME 1 / FRAME 1
ANSWERS:

1. b (Genesis 4:8)

2. c (Ruth 4:9–10)

3. b (Genesis 22:13)

4. c (1 Corinthians 15:4)

5. a (Genesis 6:14, 22)

6. d (the Bible's table of contents)

7. d (Matthew 10:3)

8. c (1 Samuel 4:18–19, 21)

9. a (Job 1:18–19)

10. b (Acts 7:54–60)

Spare. a (2 Samuel 1:25)

GAME 1/FRAME 2
ANSWERS:

1. b (Acts 28:3)

2. a (Judges 4:21)

3. d (Job 2:11; 42:7)

4. d (Revelation 20:2–3)

5. b (John 18:10)

6. a (Exodus 7:15–19)

7. c (Ephesians 6:17)

8. c (Genesis 16:15)

9. d (Isaiah 39:2–7)

10. b (John 11:35)

Spare. d (Luke 6:39)

GAME 1/FRAME 3 ANSWERS:

1. c (Joshua 7:20–22)

2. a (2 Kings 17:1–6)

3. c (the Bible's table of contents—
      1 Timothy, 2 Timothy)

4. d (James 1:13–14)

5. a (1 Kings 19:19–21)

6. c (Esther 3:6)

7. a (2 Samuel 11:4–15, 23–24)

8. d (Ephesians 2:8–9)

9. a (Revelation 3:1–6)

10. a (Luke 23:45)

Spare. d (Genesis 1:26)

GAME 1/FRAME 4
ANSWERS:

1. b (Acts 22:3)

2. a (Genesis 25:21–25)

3. d (Ezekiel 1:3, 16–18)

4. c (James 3:17)

5. c (Leviticus 11:3–7—cloven hoofs and chewing the cud)

6. a (2 Kings 1:8)

7. b (Acts 10:5–6)

8. b (Mark 4:3–8)

9. a (Genesis 19:36–37)

10. a (Luke 10:39–40)

Spare. d (John 18:38)

GAME 1/FRAME 5
ANSWERS:

1. d (Esther 7:3–6)

2. c (Genesis 41:2–6)

3. c (Hebrews 11:1)

4. b (2 Timothy 1:5)

5. d (Numbers 1:26–27—74,600)

6. a (Matthew 4:23)

7. a (1 Kings 20:35–36)

8. b (Judges 4:8–9)

9. c (Acts 18:2–3)

10. d (2 Kings 2:11)

Spare. c (Matthew 5:1–2; 7:7)

GAME 1/FRAME 6
ANSWERS:

1) a (Philemon 1:1, 15–16)

2) a (Genesis 35:26)

3) b (Acts 19:34)

4) c (1 Samuel 17:49–50)

5) b (the Bible's table of contents)

6) b (Romans 1:25)

7) a (1 Samuel 7:10–12)

8) d (Hebrews 13:8)

9) b (Genesis 1:31–2:2)

10) d (Job 39:13–17)

Spare. c (Luke 1:46)

GAME 1/FRAME 7
ANSWERS:

1) a (Numbers 11:3)

2) d (John 8:6)

3) d (Jeremiah 36:22–23)

4) d (2 Kings 25:27–30)

5) c (Ephesians 6:18)

6) a (Revelation 21:12)

7) a (Genesis 40:5)

8) b (John 6:35)

9) c (Numbers 15:38–40)

10) c (Genesis 6:8)

Spare. b (Matthew 22:21)

GAME 1/FRAME 8 ANSWERS:

1. a (Numbers 4:4–20)

2. c (Acts 2:22–23)

3. b (Ruth 1:20)

4. a (John 3:29)

5. d (1 Samuel 1:20)

6. c (Acts 16:25)

7. b (one chapter long)

8. c (Revelation 8:2)

9. d (James 1:13–14)

10. b (1 Kings 3:25)

Spare. a (1 Kings 18:27)

GAME 1/FRAME 9
ANSWERS:

1. a (Luke 18:11–14)

2. a (Romans 3:23)

3. d (Genesis 47:7)

4. b (1 Samuel 3:3–10)

5. b (Judges 21:20–21)

6. d (Luke 24:1–3, 13–15)

7. c (Esther 2:7)

8. b (Revelation 21:21)

9. c (Genesis 1:20–23)

10. a (Acts 9:8–9)

Spare. c (John 19:15)

GAME 1/FRAME 10
ANSWERS:

1. a (Matthew 17:16–20)

2. d (Revelation 20:15)

3. d (1 Samuel 16:11)

4. c (Ezekiel 1:10)

5. a (2 Kings 2:21)

6. c (Daniel 4:25)

7. a (Acts 9:2)

8. b (1 Samuel 14:27)

9. c (Ephesians 6:13)

10. b (Acts 10:6)

Spare. d (Galatians 6:7)

GAME 1/BONUS BALL 1 ANSWERS:

1. c (the Bible's table of contents)

2. b (Revelation 3:7–10)

3. a (Judges 6:37–40)

4. d (Genesis 10:6)

5. a (Genesis 2:7, 19)

6. c (Mark 14:25)

7. b (1 Kings 11:2–5)

8. c (Luke 13:11)

9. d (Acts 11:26)

10. b (Daniel 2:5–8)

Spare. a (2 Kings 22:3, 13)

GAME 1/BONUS BALL 2
ANSWERS:

1. d (Esther 2:7)

2. b (Genesis 44:2, 12)

3. a (Acts 15:40)

4. a (Genesis 2:2)

5. c (Luke 1:3)

6. b (Acts 12:23)

7. c (Luke 22:44)

8. d (2 Kings 25:25)

9. a (the Bible's table of contents)

10. c (2 Kings 22:8)

GAME 2/FRAME 1
ANSWERS:

1. d (Matthew 13:31–34)

2. a (Joshua 22:12, 26–28, 33)

3. d (Acts 18:11)

4. b (2 Kings 4:41)

5. b (Judges 15:15)

6. c (1 Peter 1:18–19)

7. a (Numbers 1:34–35—32,200)

8. a (Mark 10:46–51)

9. a (Mark 11:12–14, 20–21)

10. c (Genesis 3:13)

Spare. b (Exodus 5:1)

GAME 2/FRAME 2
ANSWERS:

1. b (2 Timothy 1:5)

2. a (Joshua 2:6)

3. d (John 3:1–2)

4. b (Genesis 37:27)

5. b (Matthew 2:3)

6. c (2 Kings 1:2)

7. c (Genesis 17:13)

8. b (Acts 23:8)

9. a (Genesis 27:1)

10. b (John 19:20)

Spare. d (Daniel 5:5, 25)

GAME 2/FRAME 3
ANSWERS:

1. a (Genesis 39:14)

2. d (Acts 18:24)

3. a (2 Kings 11:1–3)

4. b (Exodus 3:1–2)

5. c (Luke 1:41, 44, 60; 3:2–3)

6. d (Ephesians 6:5–6)

7. d (2 Kings 6:4–6)

8. b (Mark 3:17)

9. d (Matthew 28:5–7)

10. a (Joshua 9:4–6)

Spare. d (Luke 2:13–14)

GAME 2/FRAME 4
ANSWERS:

1. b (Luke 18:15)

2. c (Genesis 6:14)

3. a (Colossians 4:14)

4. b (Genesis 1:14–19)

5. b (Numbers 20:12)

6. d (Luke 23:9)

7. c (Psalm 42:1 and attribution)

8. d (Judges 12:5–6)

9. c (Revelation 21:2–3)

10. a (2 Kings 2:17)

Spare. a (Isaiah 1:18)

GAME 2/FRAME 5
ANSWERS:

1. b (Daniel 3:24–25)

2. a (Luke 18:5)

3. b (1 Kings 18:31–38)

4. d (Genesis 7:23)

5. c (Matthew 27:32)

6. c (James 3:2–10)

7. b (2 Samuel 17:17–18)

8. a (Luke 23:6–7)

9. c (Acts 4:36)

10. d (Joel 2:32)

Spare. a (Ephesians 4:26)

GAME 2/FRAME 6
ANSWERS:

1. a (Matthew 25:1–3)

2. c (Jude 1:1)

3. d (1 Kings 3:5–9)

4. c (Leviticus 11:9–12—fins and scales)

5. b (Isaiah 38:8)

6. b (Numbers 17:8)

7. c (Revelation 11:3)

8. a (Revelation 21:1–2, 14)

9. c (1 Kings 11:3)

10. a (2 Kings 1:9–14)

Spare. d (Luke 6:31)

GAME 2/FRAME 7
ANSWERS:

1. d (Acts 19:24–29)

2. b (Luke 13:14)

3. c (Exodus 15:22–23)

4. a (1 Samuel 6:7)

5. a (2 Peter 3:9)

6. b (Numbers 4:24–26)

7. b (Philemon 1:1)

8. b (1 Samuel 16:19)

9. c (Acts 15:37–39)

10. b (Genesis 7:24)

Spare. c (Exodus 16:3)

GAME 2/FRAME 8
ANSWERS:

1. c (Luke 5:19)

2. b (Exodus 25:10)

3. a (Exodus 14:30)

4. d (1 Samuel 13:9–13)

5. c (Revelation 16:1, 17)

6. a (Matthew 1; Luke 3)

7. b (Exodus 16:31)

8. c (Genesis 9:22)

9. a (Acts 8:32; Isaiah 53:7–8)

10. a (1 Kings 10:23)

Spare. c (Daniel 6:20)

GAME 2/FRAME 9
ANSWERS:

b (1 Kings 1:5; 2 Samuel 3:2–4)

a (Luke 16:20–22)

c (Luke 10:30–37)

d (Exodus 17:5–6)

c (Joshua 6:2, 20)

b (2 Peter 3:12)

b (Acts 18:2)

c (Numbers 4:29–33)

a (1 Samuel 11:1–11)

b (Mark 1:9, 12–13)

Spare. d (John 3:4)

GAME 2/FRAME 10
ANSWERS:

1. c (150 chapters)

2. a (Matthew 12:36)

3. c (Luke 1:59, 63–64)

4. c (Genesis 5:5)

5. c (2 Samuel 24:13–15)

6. d (Acts 9:1–2)

7. b (2 Samuel 14:25–26)

8. b (Matthew 28:18)

9. a (Matthew 20:20–21)

10. c (Judges 4:7)

Spare. d (Matthew 19:24)

GAME 2/BONUS BALL 1
ANSWERS:

1. d (Deuteronomy 34:5–6)

2. b (1 Samuel 16:10–11, 13)

3. c (Exodus 32:15–16)

4. b (Matthew 17:24–27)

5. d (Genesis 19:36–38)

6. d (John 20:31)

7. a (Matthew 14:29)

8. d (Mark 14:50)

9. c (Joshua 6:5)

10. a (Ephesians 6:17)

Spare. a (Acts 5:29)

GAME 2/BONUS BALL 2 ANSWERS:

1. c (Joshua 3:13)

2. d (Revelation 4:8; Genesis 1:1–2)

3. a (Proverbs 22:2)

4. c (only 13 verses)

5. b (Mark 1:7)

6. a (Psalm 51:4 and attribution)

7. d (Joshua 13:3)

8. c (Genesis 8:6–7)

9. b (John 19:17)

10. a (Titus 1:5)

GAME 3/FRAME 1
ANSWERS:

1. b (John 2:9, 11)

2. a (1 Kings 10:27)

3. c (Genesis 13:12)

4. d (John 2:13–16)

5. a (Genesis 20:2)

6. b (Luke 12:16–21)

7. d (1 John 4:8)

8. c (Luke 6:13)

9. c (Exodus 7:15–12:32)

10. c (1 Kings 16:30–31)

Spare. d (Acts 26:27–28)

GAME 3/FRAME 2
ANSWERS:

1. c (Ephesians 6:15)

2. a (Acts 9:7)

3. d (Exodus 16:31)

4. b (1 Samuel 14:24, 27, 43)

5. a (Psalm 8:1 and attribution)

6. a (Matthew 2:13–15)

7. c (1 Kings 21:5–16)

8. b (Numbers 14:22–23)

9. b (Acts 21:39)

10. a (Hebrews 10:31)

Spare. a (Joshua 24:15)

GAME 3/FRAME 3
ANSWERS:

1. a (Numbers 14:36–37)

2. d (Acts 15:28–29)

3. b (Daniel 3:19–23)

4. c (Luke 8:2)

5. b (2 Peter 3:8)

6. b (1 Samuel 15:2–3, 9)

7. a (Matthew 1:18–25)

8. b (Genesis 19:26)

9. b (Isaiah 6:3; Revelation 4:8)

10. a (1 Samuel 31:4)

Spare. d (Mark 14:30, 38)

GAME 3/FRAME 4
ANSWERS:

1. c (Acts 13:9)

2. c (Psalm 139:13–16)

3. a (Luke 8:23–24)

4. c (Psalm 46:10 and attribution)

5. b (Genesis 34:2)

6. a (Revelation 21:22–23)

7. d (1 Kings 22:39)

8. c (Acts 2:41; 4:4)

9. a (Hebrews 9:27)

10. a (Judges 17:6; 21:25)

Spare. b (Genesis 4:9)

GAME 3/FRAME 5
ANSWERS:

1. b (Numbers 22:4–8)

2. d (John 2:2–10)

3. b (Matthew 8:31–32)

4. a (Joshua 2:3–4)

5. a (Amos 1:1)

6. d (Luke 21:1–4)

7. b (Genesis 1:12–13)

8. c (Acts 20:9)

9. b (Ephesians 6:16)

10. c (Joshua 18:28)

Spare. d (Genesis 11:6–7)

GAME 3/FRAME 6
ANSWERS:

1. c (Genesis 6:13–17)

2. a (Acts 2:1–4)

3. a (Hosea 1:2)

4. b (1 Kings 19:19–21)

5. c (1 Corinthians 15:3–4)

6. c (Galatians 2:11–12)

7. a (Judges 7:2–3)

8. b (Matthew 13:22)

9. b (Matthew 4:18)

10. d (2 Kings 9:33)

Spare. a (Esther 4:15–16)

GAME 3/FRAME 7 ANSWERS:

1. a (Judges 3:9)

2. d (Leviticus 11:29–30)

3. c (Acts 1:1–3)

4. b (Jonah 2:1, 10)

5. c (John 19:38–39)

6. c (Acts 5:5, 10)

7. c (Matthew 27:66)

8. b (1 Samuel 6:11)

9. a (Acts 12:10)

10. d (Joshua 10:13)

Spare. d (Luke 12:16–19)

GAME 3/FRAME 8
ANSWERS:

1. d (John 20:11, 15)

2. d (Psalm 119:105 and attribution)

3. b (Genesis 4:1)

4. b (Exodus 7:14–11:5)

5. a (Acts 16:1)

6. c (Acts 18:2)

7. b (Nehemiah 1:11; 2:1)

8. a (Matthew 26:63–64)

9. c (1 Kings 16:24)

10. d (John 21:25)

Spare. b (Luke 2:25–30)

GAME 3/FRAME 9
ANSWERS:

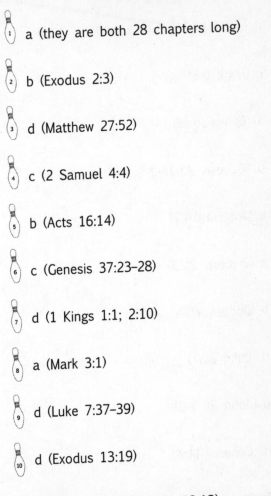

1. a (they are both 28 chapters long)

2. b (Exodus 2:3)

3. d (Matthew 27:52)

4. c (2 Samuel 4:4)

5. b (Acts 16:14)

6. c (Genesis 37:23–28)

7. d (1 Kings 1:1; 2:10)

8. a (Mark 3:1)

9. d (Luke 7:37–39)

10. d (Exodus 13:19)

Spare. b (1 Corinthians 13:13)

GAME 3/FRAME 10 ANSWERS:

1. a (John 14:26; Ephesians 1:13; 4:30)

2. c (Mark 6:3)

3. a (Ephesians 6:14)

4. d (Genesis 42:32–36)

5. b (Joshua 14:2)

6. a (2 Kings 2:23)

7. b (Judges 7:7)

8. d (Luke 2:37)

9. b (John 20:5–6)

10. d (Genesis 11:4)

Spare. c (John 19:30)

GAME 3/BONUS BALL 1 ANSWERS:

1. d (1 Kings 5:5–6)

2. d (John 20:7)

3. c (2 Samuel 12:15–18)

4. a (Exodus 17:9–13)

5. d (2 Kings 25:2–7)

6. b (Matthew 26:14–16)

7. b (Philemon 1:10, 15–16)

8. c (Acts 2:1–4)

9. a (2 Kings 5:9–14)

10. c (Luke 2:43–50)

Spare. d (Genesis 1:3)

GAME 3/BONUS BALL 2 ANSWERS:

1. d (Acts 10:11–15)

2. a (Genesis 38:24–27)

3. a (Luke 11:29–30)

4. a (Psalm 23:1 and attribution)

5. c (Exodus 14:21)

6. d (Matthew 1:3–16)

7. c (1 Kings 17:13)

8. b (Judges 6:32)

9. c (Luke 1:57–63)

10. a (Philemon 1:22)

GAME 4/FRAME 1
ANSWERS:

1. c (Proverbs 31:10–31)

2. a (Numbers 21:23–24)

3. b (Genesis 17:5)

4. c (Luke 23:32)

5. a (Amos 7:14)

6. d (Leviticus 11:20–23)

7. b (Matthew 13:10–15)

8. c (Matthew 13:20–21)

9. b (Luke 11:14–15)

10. c (Genesis 35:23)

Spare. b (1 Corinthians 11:23–25)

GAME 4/FRAME 2
ANSWERS:

1. b (1 Samuel 1:20)

2. b (Genesis 25:24; Hebrews 11:5)

3. d (Genesis 25:26)

4. c (Matthew 26:59–60)

5. a (Joshua 3:14–16)

6. b (Matthew 13:38)

7. d (Acts 16:1)

8. d (Ezekiel 1:1–3)

9. b (Joshua 10:16)

10. d (Matthew 24:36–37)

Spare. a (Isaiah 6:8)

GAME 4/FRAME 3
ANSWERS:

1. c (1 Corinthians 13:4–8)

2. c (Revelation 10:8–10)

3. a (1 Samuel 22:12–18)

4. d (2 Kings 4:18–19)

5. c (Acts 14:1, 12)

6. d (Psalm 100, attribution)

7. a (Luke 15:7, 10, 32)

8. a (Ezekiel 4:15)

9. a (Proverbs 22:13)

10. a (2 Kings 2:11)

Spare. c (Job 1:20–21)

GAME 4/FRAME 4
ANSWERS:

1. c (1 Samuel 5:4)

2. b (Genesis 32:28)

3. a (Revelation 21:16)

4. b (Genesis 8:11)

5. c (Acts 21:26–28)

6. a (1 Samuel 25:10, 37–38)

7. d (Ezekiel 37:1–10)

8. a (Acts 12:15–16)

9. b (Revelation 22:1–2)

10. a (Proverbs 30:1)

Spare. b (Luke 2:10–11)

GAME 4/FRAME 5
ANSWERS:

1. a (2 Samuel 16:5–8)

2. b (Daniel 6:16)

3. d (Ezra 4:4–24)

4. b (the Bible's table of contents)

5. d (Revelation 22:2)

6. b (Esther 1:1; 2:17)

7. b (1 Samuel 18:8–9)

8. c (2 Kings 4:3–7)

9. b (Exodus 32:20)

10. b (Acts 4:36)

Spare. c (Luke 22:42)

GAME 4/FRAME 6
ANSWERS:

1. a (1 Kings 19:2–8)

2. c (Acts 4:31)

3. a (2 Kings 19:5–7)

4. a (Joshua 18:1)

5. c (Genesis 6:14)

6. b (John 4:6, 17–18)

7. c (Matthew 27:17–19)

8. c (Genesis 1:26, 31)

9. c (Genesis 48:17–19)

10. d (Matthew 13:23)

Spare. a (Isaiah 5:20)

GAME 4/FRAME 7 ANSWERS:

1. a (2 Samuel 11:3)

2. b (Revelation 20:9)

3. c (Proverbs 1:20)

4. b (Mark 15:9–11)

5. b (2 Samuel 11:14–15)

6. d (1 Samuel 21:13)

7. d (Acts 4:36)

8. c (1 Kings 17:1–4)

9. c (Matthew 13:38)

10. a (Psalm 103:12 and attribution)

Spare. c (Matthew 27:46)

GAME 4/FRAME 8
ANSWERS:

1) c (Exodus 38:1–2)

2) c (Matthew 2:1)

3) a (Genesis 45:3)

4) b (Revelation 20:8)

5) a (Joshua 18:1; 1 Samuel 1:24, 28)

6) d (Acts 2:2)

7) c (Exodus 16:8–13)

8) b (Esther 1:10–11)

9) b (Acts 14:12)

10) c (Leviticus 11:13–19)

Spare. b (1 Corinthians 3:6)

GAME 4/FRAME 9
ANSWERS:

1. a (Leviticus 10:1–2)

2. b (the Bible's table of contents)

3. c (Judges 3:15)

4. b (Mark 15:17)

5. c (Acts 2:5–8, 15)

6. a (Joshua 4:3)

7. a (Revelation 10:10)

8. a (Genesis 35:25)

9. b (Exodus 34:1)

10. d (Acts 1:26)

Spare. d (John 13:38)

GAME 4/FRAME 10 ANSWERS:

1. a (1 Samuel 1:13)

2. d (Genesis 36:1)

3. d (Numbers 35:11–12)

4. c (Acts 3:2–8; 4:22)

5. d (Acts 1:11)

6. b (Psalm 90:1, 12)

7. c (James 1:19)

8. a (Luke 1:59–63)

9. c (Exodus 18:17–23)

10. c (Genesis 37:3)

Spare. a (1 Samuel 3:10)

GAME 4/BONUS BALL 1 ANSWERS:

1. a (Numbers 11:31–34)

2. b (Leviticus 7:23–27)

3. b (Acts 13:2)

4. c (Genesis 9:13–16)

5. d (Revelation 2:1–7)

6. a (Joshua 8:2)

7. c (Numbers 16:1–5, 31–35)

8. a (Matthew 13:19)

9. a (Genesis 35:24)

10. c (John 1:23)

Spare. d (Matthew 4:1–4; Deuteronomy 8:3)

GAME 4/BONUS BALL 2 ANSWERS:

1. d (Joshua 6:21–23)

2. a (Lamentations 1:1–4)

3. c (Genesis 17:15)

4. b (John 6:8–9)

5. a (Leviticus 16:21–22)

6. b (Matthew 26:47–49)

7. b (Exodus 28:3)

8. c (Numbers 27:1–4)

9. d (John 1:1)

10. a (Revelation 3:14–16)